The PSPP Guide
Expanded Edition

The PSPP Guide:
An Introduction to Statistical Analysis (Expanded Edition)

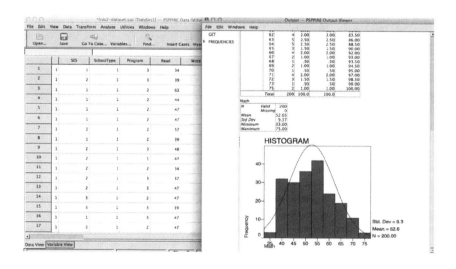

Christopher P. Halter

CreativeMinds Press Group

San Diego, CA

The PSPP Guide

Copyright © 2014 by Christopher P. Halter

http://creativemindspress.weebly.com

ISBN: 069231363X
ISBN-13: 978-0692313633

ACKNOWLEDGMENTS

Whether knowingly or unknowingly, those of us using technology owe a great deal to the open source software community. It is through projects such as PSPP, OpenOffice, Linux, and others that useful applications can be freely distributed. The programmers who make up this community of professionals offer their time and effort for nothing more than the ability to share something worthwhile with the rest of us.

Thank you.

CONTENTS

"An approximate answer to the right problem is worth a good deal more than an exact answer to an approximate problem." -- John Tukey

Chapter 1
An Introduction to the Expanded Guide

Notes about the statistics guide

The purpose of this guide is to assist the novice social science and educational researcher in interpreting statistical output data using the PSPP Statistical Analysis application. Through the examples and guidance you will be able to select, apply, and use a statistical test's output table.

There are two PSPP Guides to choose from, both have very similar examples and explanations. This guide (PSPP Expanded) contains examples described at a much deeper level than the Basic Edition. It also contains a description of Factor Analysis, a data reduction technique. The second guide (PSPP Basic) contains the foundational statistical analysis methods and explanations to help the novice researcher get started.

The Expanded Guide goes into more depth about the uses and limitations of each statistical test described, i.e. Chi-square, t-Test, ANOVA, Correlation, and Regressions. The ANOVA description included procedures for conducting the One-Way ANOVA with Planned Contrasts so that you may test a specific hypothesis concerning group interactions. Factor Analysis has been included in this guide as a valuable procedure for data reduction.

The sample window views and output tables shown in this guide were created by PSPP 0.8.2, the graphical user interface version of PSPP.

PSPP is officially described as a "replacement" application for IBM's Statistical Package for the Social Sciences (SPSS). However, PSPP does not have any official acronymic expansion. The developers of PSPP have some suggestions, such as;

- Perfect Statistics Professionally Presented.
- Probabilities Sometimes Prevent Problems.
- People Should Prefer PSPP.

This guide suggests using several open source applications, including PSPP (statistical analysis) and OpenOffice (productivity). You will also find references to online statistical information and calculators.

The examples shown in this guide represent a subset of the data obtained in the 1988-2000 High School & Beyond (HS&B) study commissioned by the Center on Education Policy (CEP). The sample datasets contain 200 cases and are intended to provide statistical analysis practice and not to draw any conclusions about the sample population.

Notes about the data set

The High School & Beyond study was commissioned by the Center on Education Policy (CEP) and conducted by researcher Harold Wenglinsky. The study was based on the statistical analyses of a nationally representative, longitudinal database of students and schools (the National Educational Longitudinal Study of 1988-2000, or NELS). The study focused on a sample of low-income students from inner-city high schools. The study compared achievement and other education-related outcomes for students in different types of public and private schools, including comprehensive public high schools (the typical model for the traditional high school); public magnet schools and "schools of choice;" various types of Catholic parochial schools and other religious schools; and independent, secular private schools. The High School and Beyond (HS&B) study included two cohorts: the 1980 senior class, and the 1980 sophomore class.

To learn more about the High School & Beyond research study visit
http://nces.ed.gov/surveys/hsb/

Data files that have been used in this book can be downloaded from our website.
http://creativemindspress.weebly.com/resources-for-pspp.html

The Philosophy Behind This Book and the Open Source Community

This book began as my own attempt to find a practical way to teach introductory statistical analysis to doctoral students in our program. The course would often come early in the training of our students prior to the start of their own data collection or research study. They would purchase a license for one of the major proprietary statistical analysis packages, typically a six month or one-year license. Unfortunately, by the time they had data to analyze the software license would have expired.

So began my search for an alternative that would be useful in learning basic analysis skills and capable of performing statistical analysis tests. This brought me to PSPP, a part of the GNU Project. This open source computer community has developed a powerful software package that is effective and easy to use. Another key feature of the open source group is that the software is distributed free of charge.

As I explored the software I found that it worked very well with another open source project, OpenOffice. This application suite is capable of creating word processing documents, spreadsheets, and presentations. Together, PSPP and OpenOffice provide the novice researcher with the tools to learn and explore while saving them from spending a lot of money on proprietary software.

This guide is not intended to be a course on statistics or the mathematics behind statistical analysis. With the advent of statistical analysis applications anyone with a computer can run statistical analysis on any dataset. The intention of this guide is to provide the novice researcher with a step-by-step guide to using these powerful analysis tools and the confidence to read and interpret output tables in order to guide their own research.

Chapter 2
Overview of Statistical Analysis in Social Science

Why use statistics in Social Science research?

Everyone loves a good story. Rich narratives, interesting characters, and the unfolding of events draw us into the story and makes us invested in how it ends. Qualitative research methods are well suited to uncover theses stories. However, we should not ignore the power and use of quantitative methods.

One of the assumptions made about quantitative research methods is that they merely deal with numbers. And let's face it, to many of us, numbers are quite boring. A well-constructed data table or beautifully drawn graph does not capture the imagination of most readers. But appropriately used quantitative methods can uncover subtle differences, point out inconsistencies, or bring up more questions that beg to be answered.

In short, thoughtful quantitative methods can help guide and shape the qualitative story. This union of rich narratives and statistical evidence is at the heart of any good mixed methods study. The researcher uses the data to guide the narrative. Together these methods can reveal a more complete and complex account of the topic.

What is Continuous and Categorical Data?

Within statistical analysis we often talk about data as being either continuous or categorical. This distinction is important since it guides us towards appropriate methods that are used for each kind of data set. Depending on the kind of data you have there are specific statistical techniques available for you to use with that data.

Mark Twain (1804-1881) is often credited with describing the three types of lies as "lies, damn lies, and statistics". This phrase is still often used in association with our view of statistics. This may be due to the fact that one could manipulate statistical analysis to give whatever outcome is being sought. Poor statistics has also been used to support weak or inconsistent claims. This does not mean that the statistics is at fault, but rather a researcher who used statistical methods inappropriately. As researchers we must take great care in employing proper methods with our data.

Continuous data can be thought of as "scaled data". The numbers may have been obtained from some sort of assessment or from some counting activity. A common example of continuous data is test scores. If we can plot the data with a line graph then it is probably continuous data.

Some examples of continuous data include;
- The time it takes to complete a task
- A student's test scores
- Time of day that someone goes to bed
- The weight or height of a 2nd grade student

All of these examples can be thought of as rational numbers. For those of us who have not been in an Algebra class for a number of years, rational numbers can be represented as fractions, which in turn can be represented as decimals. Rational numbers can still be represented as whole numbers as well.

A subset of this sort of data can be called discrete data. Discrete data is obtained from counting things. They are represented by whole numbers. Some examples of discreet numbers include;

- The number of courses a student takes each year
- The number of people living in a household
- The number of languages spoken by someone
- The number of turns taken by an individual

Categorical data is another type of important statistical data, and one that is often used in social science research. As the name implies, categorical data is comprised of categories or the names of things that we are interested in studying. In working with statistical methods we often transform the names of our categories into numbers.

An example of this process is when we collect information about the primary languages spoken at home by students in our class. We may have found that the primary home languages are English, Spanish, French, and Cantonese. We may convert this data into numbers for analysis.

Table 1: Primary Home Language Code Book

Language Spoken	Code
English	1
Spanish	2
French	3
Cantonese	4

In the above example the numbers assigned to the categories do not signify any differences or order in the languages. The numbers used here are "nominal" or used to represent names.

Another example of categorical data could be the grade level of a high school student. In this case we may be interested in high school freshmen, sophomores, juniors, and seniors. Assigning a numerical label to these categories may make our analysis simpler.

Table 2: High School Grade Levels

Grade Level	Code
Freshman	1
Sophomore	2
Junior	3
Senior	4

In this example, again the numbers are just representing the names of the high school level, however they do have an order. "Freshman" comes prior to "Sophomore", which is prior to "Junior", and also "Senior". This sort of categorical data can be described as ordinal, or representing an order.

What kind of data comes from questionnaires?

Many questionnaires will contain open ended or free-response questions as well as Likert-scale questions. This latter data source can be very beneficial in social science research and provide the researcher with a wealth of information and data. Likert-scale responses can be used to measure preference or agreement with a statement.

But are the responses on a questionnaire categorical or continuous?

The answer to this question is not as easy as it might seem. Different sectors of the field will have different responses to this question. You will find some referring to this data as categorical and others referring to it as continuous. The disagreement seems to stem from our own definition of continuous data.

When we think about continuous data, a key feature is that the numbers have a measured or scaled distance from one another. So when we examine the points along our scale we can find a precise way to describe the difference between one point to the next.

For example, the height of students in a classroom could be scaled data. When we describe one student as being 4 feet tall, another as 3 feet tall, and a third as 3.5 feet tall, the differences between those points is measured and precise. We can infer a standard difference between the three.

If we have data such as the one used in the high school level example, the difference between a freshman, a sophomore, and a junior is not as precise. The students at all three of those levels will have various skills and abilities, they will have taken different course sequences, and they have differing credits gained in school. Even within these groups there are still differences in courses, skills, and credits achieved. So there is not a defined scale that makes one group different from the next or provides for differences within the grouping.

So when we have a questionnaire that asks about one's feeling to a specific topic, are the differences between those responses along a measured scale and do the responses have similarities about the meaning?

A typical Likert-scale questionnaire might ask a range of questions in which the responses can be "disagree, neither disagree or agree, and agree". We would provide a numbered response scale to make the selections easier for our participants.

Table 3: Sample Likert Scale

Simple Likert-scale direction
Please respond to the following questions using the scale provided;
Disagree – 1
Neither disagree nor agree – 2
Agree - 3

So does this sort of data have a measured, scaled difference between the responses? That is a question that each researcher must answer and justify before employing any statistical analysis methods.

How do we tell them apart and why is it important?

It is important to recognize the sort of data that is being used in the research analysis process. A researcher should ask;

- Does my data represent information that is continuous (a rational number) or is it categorical (names and labels)?
- Does this represent test scores or evaluations?
- Does this data represent something that has been counted?
- Is the interval between the data points a regular, measured interval?
- Could this data be represented with a linear graph?
- Does this data represent the names of something?
- Do the data points represent the order of objects?
- Are the data points opinions?
- Are there differences within the data categories?
- Are there irregular differences between the data points?

Depending on whether a researcher is using categorical or continuous data, there are specific statistical methods available. Table 4 represents some of the most common statistical methods in social science research and the data associated with the method.

Table 4: Common Statistical Methods

	Statistical Method	Representation and Use
Descriptive Statistics	Normal Distribution	Graphs
	Central Tendencies	Mean, Median, Mode
	Variance	Standard Deviation
	Charts and Graphs	Histogram, Pie Chart, Stem & Leaf Plots, Scatterplots

Inferential Statistics	Chi-square	Differences or relationships between categorical data
	t-Test	Differences or relationships between continuous data with two groups
	ANOVA	Differences or relationships between continuous data with more than 2 groups
	Correlation	Associations between continuous data
	Regression	Modeling associations between continuous data
	Factor Analysis	Factor grouping within categorical or continuous data. Data reduction.

Parametric versus Non-Parametric Data

Our data can also be classified as either parametric or nonparametric. This term refers to the distribution of data points. Parametric data will have a "normal distribution" that is generally shaped like the typical bell curve. Non-parametric data does not have this normal distribution curve.

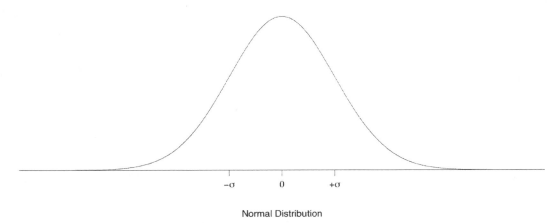

Normal Distribution

Figure 1: Normal Distribution Curve

Depending on the distribution of your data, various statistical analysis techniques are available to use. Some methods are designed for parametric data while other methods are better suited for non-parametric data distributions.

Table 5: Sample Statistics based on Data Distribution

	Parametric	**Non-Parametric**
Data Distribution	Normal	Any
Variance within Data	Homogenous	Any
Typical Data Type	Continuous (Ratio or Interval)	Categorical (Ordinal or Nominal)
Benefits of the data	More powerful, able to draw stronger conclusions	Simpler to use
Statistical Tests		
Correlations	Pearson	Spearman
Relationships with 2 groups	t-Test	Mann-Whitney or Wilcoxon Test
Relationships with >2 groups	ANOVA	Kruskal-Wallis or Friedman's Test

In choosing a statistical method we must consider both the character of the data as well as the distribution of our data. The character, or data type, can be described as nominal, ordinal, ratio, or interval. The distribution can be described as parametric or non-parametric. These data features will lead us to selecting the most appropriate statistical method for our analysis of the data.

Throughout this guide the examples will come from our sample data set that contains both categorical and continuous data that is generally parametric in nature.

P-Value

What is a P-value?

In statistical analysis the way we measure the significance of any given test is with the P-value. This value indicates the probability of obtaining the same statistical test result by chance. Our calculated p-values are compared against some predetermined significance level. The most common significance levels are the 95% Significance Level, represented by a p-value of 0.05, and the 99% Significance Level, represented by a p-value of 0.01. A significance level of 95%, or 0.05, indicates that we are accepting the risk of being wrong 20% of the time, or 1 out of every 20 times. A significance level of 99%, or 0.01, indicates that we risk being wrong only 1 out of every 100 times. The most common significance level used in the Social Sciences is 95%, so we are looking for p-values < 0.05 in our test results.

However, in statistical analysis we are not looking to prove our test hypothesis with the p-value. We are actually trying to reject the Null Hypothesis.

What is the Null Hypothesis?

In statistical testing the results are always comparing two competing hypothesis. The null hypothesis is often the dull, boring hypothesis stating that there is no difference between the test populations or conditions. The null hypothesis tells us that whatever phenomenon we were observing had no or very little impact. On the other hand we have the alternative, or researcher's hypothesis. This is the hypothesis that we are rooting for, the one that we want to be accepted in most cases. It is the result we often want to find since it often indicates that there are differences between populations or conditions so then we can take that next step to explain those differences or examine them more closely.

When we perform a statistical test, the p-value helps determine the significance of the test and the validity of the claim being made. The claim that is always "on trial" here is the null hypothesis. When the p-value is found to be statistically significant, $p < 0.05$, or that it is highly statistically significant, $p < 0.01$, then we can conclude that the differences, relationships, or associations found in the observed data are very unlikely to occur if the null hypothesis is actually true. Therefore the researcher can "reject the null hypothesis". If you reject the null hypothesis then the alternative hypothesis must be accepted. And this is often what we want as researchers.

The only question that the p-value addresses is whether or not the experiment or data provide enough evidence to reasonably reject null hypothesis. The p-value or calculated probability is the estimated probability of rejecting the null hypothesis of a study question when that null hypothesis is actually true. In other words, it measures the probability that you will be wrong in rejecting the null hypothesis. And all of this is decided based on our predetermined significance level, in most cases the 95% level or $p < 0.05$.

Let's look at an example. Suppose your school purchases a SAT Prep curriculum in the hopes that this will raise the SAT test scores of your students. Some students are enrolled in the prep course while others are not enrolled in the prep course. At the end of the course all your students take the SAT test and their resulting test scores are compared.

In this example our null hypothesis would be that "the SAT prep curriculum had no impact on student test scores". This result would be bad news considering how much time, effort, and money was invested in the test prep. The alternative hypothesis is that the prep curriculum did have an impact on the test scores, and hopefully the impact was to raise those scores. Our predetermined significance level is 95%. After using a statistical test we find that the p-value is 0.02 which is in deed less than 0.05. We can reject the null hypothesis. Now that we have rejected the null hypothesis the only other option is to accept the alternative hypothesis, specifically that the scores are significantly different.

This result does NOT imply a "meaningful" or "important" difference in the data. That conclusion is for you to decide when considering the real-world relevance of your result. So again, statistical analysis is not the end point in research, but a meaningful beginning point to help the researcher identify important and fruitful directions suggested by the data.

It has been suggested that the idea of "rejecting the null hypothesis" has very little meaning for social science research. The null hypothesis always states that there are "no differences" to be found within your data. Can we really find NO DIFFERENCES in the data? Are the results that we find between two groups ever going to be identical to one another?

The practical answer to these questions is "No". There will always be differences present in our data. What we are really asking is whether or not those differences have any statistical significance. As we discussed previously, our statistical tests are aimed at producing the p-value that indicates the likelihood of having the differences occur purely by chance. And the significance level of p=0.05 is just an agreed upon value among many social scientist as the acceptable level to consider as statistically significant.

And to find that the differences within the data are statistically significant may just be a factor of having a large enough sample size to make those differences meaningful.

What does this all mean?

A small p-value (typically ≤ 0.05) indicates strong evidence against the null hypothesis, so you reject the null hypothesis. A large p-value (> 0.05) indicates weak evidence against the null hypothesis, so you fail to reject the null hypothesis. P-values very close to the cutoff (0.05) are considered to be marginal so you could go either way. But keep in mind that the choice of significance levels is arbitrary. We have selected a significance level of 95% because of the conventions used in most Social Science research. I could have easily selected a significance level of 80%, but then no one would take my results very seriously.

Relying on the p-value alone can give you a false sense of security. The p-value is also very sensitive to sample size. If a given sample size yields a p-value that is close to the significance level, increasing the sample size can often shift the p-value in a favorable direction, i.e. make the resulting value smaller.

So how can we use p-values and have a sense of the magnitude of the differences? This is where Effect Size can help.

Effect Size

What is an effect size?

Whereas statistical tests of significance tell us the likelihood that experimental results differ from chance expectations, effect-size measurements tell us the relative magnitude of those differences found within the data. Effect sizes are especially important because they allow us to compare the magnitude of results from one population or sample to the next.

Effect size is not as sensitive to sample size since it relies on standard deviation in the calculations. Effect size also allows us to move beyond the simple question of "does this work or not?" or "is there a difference or not?", but allows us to ask the question "how well does some intervention work within the given context?"

Let's take a look at an example that could, and has happened, to many of us when conducting statistical analysis. When we compare two data sets, perhaps we are looking at SAT assessment scores between a group of students who enrolled in a SAT prep course and another group of students who did not enroll in the prep course.

Suppose that the statistical test revealed a p-value of 0.043. We should be quite pleased since this value would be below our significance level of 0.05 and we could report a statistical difference exists between the group of test takers enrolled in the prep course and those who were not enrolled in the course. But what if the calculated p-value was 0.057. Does this mean that the prep course is any less effective?

So here is the bottom-line. The p-value calculation will help us decide if a difference or association has some significance that should be explored further. The effect size will give us a sense of the magnitude of any differences to help us decide if those differences have any practical meaning and are worth exploring.

So both the p-value and the effect size can be used to assist the researcher in making meaningful judgments about the differences found within our data sets.

Effect Size Calculations

I know that you were promised that this book would not contain any mathematical calculations for you to memorize. Well, that was not entirely true. Sorry.

We will need to use some simple mathematical calculations from the values produced in the PSPP output tables to determine effect size. We will take a look at the effect size calculations for Chi Square, t-Test (paired samples), t-Test (independent samples), One-Way ANOVA, and Correlations.

Calculating Effect Size for Chi Square

The Chi Square analysis has two main calculations for effect size, Phi (φ) or Cramer's Phi (φ_c). For crosstabs tables that are 2 X 2 we will use Phi. A crosstabs table that is described as 2 X 2 will have exactly 2 rows and 2 columns. With crosstabs tables that are greater than 2 X 2 we use Cramer's Phi. When we have a crosstabs table that is greater than 2 X 2 this means that output table has either 3 or more rows, 3 or more columns, or both the rows and columns have 3 or more entries.

Crosstabs Table Equal to 2 X 2

$$\phi = \sqrt{\frac{\chi 2}{N}}$$

Phi (ϕ)

In the Phi formula $\chi 2$ is equal to the Chi Square value produced by PSPP and N is the total number of observances or samples.

Crosstabs Table Greater than 2 X 2

$$\phi_c = \sqrt{\frac{\chi 2}{N(k-1)}}$$

Cramer's Phi (ϕ_c)

In the Cramer's Phi formula the $\chi 2$ is equal to the Chi Square value produced by PSPP. The N is equal to the total number of observances or samples. For k we use the lesser value from the number of rows or the number of columns.

Calculating Effect Size for t-Test (paired samples)

The Paired Samples t-Test effect size is calculated using Cohen's d

Cohen's d (d)
$$d = \frac{mean\ difference}{standard\ deviation\ (SD)}$$

or

$$d = \frac{mean_2 - mean_1}{standard\ deviation\ (SD)}$$

Calculating Effect Size for t-Test (independent samples)

The Independent Samples t-Test effect size can be calculated with either Cohen's d (in some cases referred to as Hedge's g) or the r^2 value. In this case since we will have standard deviations for two separate (independent) data sets, we must use a "pooled standard deviation" value in the equation.

Cohen's d (d)
$$d = \frac{mean\ difference}{standard\ deviation\ (SD)\ pooled}$$

or
$$d = \frac{mean_2 - mean_1}{SD\ pooled}$$

The equation to calculate the pooled standard deviation (SD_{pooled}) uses the standard deviation from each group in the equation shown below.

$$SD \text{ pooled} = \sqrt{\frac{(SD_{group1})^2 + (SD_{group2})^2}{2}}$$

The means and standard deviation values are from the t-Test (Independent samples) Output Table.

Another option to calculate the effect size for a t-Test (Independent Samples) is to use the r^2 calculation.

$$r^2 \text{ value} \qquad r^2 = \frac{t^2}{t^2 \cdot df}$$

In the r^2 formula, t is the t-value from the PSPP output table and *df* represents the degrees of freedom from the PSPP output table.

Calculating Effect Size for One-Way ANOVA

The effect size for a one-way ANOVA tests can be calculated with eta squared (η^2).

$$\text{Eta squared } (\eta^2) \qquad \eta^2 = \frac{Sum\ of\ Squares_{between\ groups}}{Sum\ of\ Squares_{total}}$$

or

$$\eta^2 = \frac{SS_{between\ groups}}{SS_{total}}$$

The Sum of Squares values are taken from the PSPP ANOVA output table.

Calculating Effect Size for Correlations

The effect size for correlations can be found by either r or r^2. Both of these values are produced in the PSPP Correlation Output Table.

Determining the Magnitude of Effect Size

Once we have calculated the effect size value we must determine if this value represents a small, medium, or large effect. Jacob Cohen (1988) suggested various effect size calculations and magnitudes in his text *Statistical Power Analysis for the Behavioral Sciences.*

Suggested Effect Size Magnitude Chart

Effect Size Calculation	Statistics Test	Small Effect	Medium Effect	Large Effect
Phi or Cramer's Phi	Chi Squared	0.1	0.3	0.5
Cohen's d	t-Test (Paired & Independent)	0.2	0.5	0.8
Eta Squared	ANOVA	0.01	0.06	0.14
r	Correlation	0.1	0.3	0.5
r^2	Correlation and t-Test (Independent)	0.01	0.09	0.25

Values from Cohen (1988) Statistical Power Analysis for the Behavioral Sciences

The values in the effect size magnitude chart can be thought of as a range of values with the numbers in each column representing the midpoint of that particular range. For example, the effect size chart for Phi suggests a small, medium, and large effect size for the values of 0.1, 0.3, and 0.5 respectively. We could think of these as ranges with the small effect for Phi ranging from 0.0 to approximately 0.2, the medium effect size ranging from approximately 0.2 to 0.4, and the large effect size ranging from approximately 0.4 and higher.

The importance of effect size can be best summed up by Gene Glass, as cited in Kline's *Beyond Significance Testing: Reforming Data Analysis Methods* in Behavioral Research, Washington DC: American Psychological Association; 2004. p. 95.

> *Statistical significance is the least interesting thing about the results. You should describe the results in terms of measures of magnitude—not just, does a treatment affect people, but how much does it affect them.*
>
> *-Gene V. Glass*

Chapter 3
The PSPP Statistical Analysis Environment

What is PSPP?

PSPP is a program for the statistical analysis of sampled data. It is particularly suited to the analysis and manipulation of very large data sets. The PSPP online guide states that in addition to statistical hypothesis tests such as t-Tests, analysis of variance and non-parametric tests, PSPP can also perform linear regressions and is a very powerful tool for recoding and sorting of data and for calculating metrics such as skewness and kurtosis.

Where do I get the application?

PSPP can be downloaded for free from many websites. Several versions that are compatible with different operating systems can be obtained directly from GNU Software's website. Select the link for your computer's operating system and follow the onscreen directions to download and install.

Figure 2: PSPP website http://www.gnu.org/software/pspp/pspp.html

Compatibility

The PSPP guide states that PSPP is designed as a free replacement for SPSS. That is to say, it behaves as experienced SPSS users would expect, and their system files and syntax files can be used in PSPP with little or no modification, and will produce similar results. PSPP supports numeric variables and string variables up to 32,767 bytes long. Variable names may be up to 255 bytes in length. This means that variable names must be less than 64 characters. There are no artificial limits on the number of variables or cases. The free PSPP application is not limited in any way.

Graphic User Interface (GUI)

Users familiar with other software may prefer the graphic user interface, which allows you to define data without needing to become familiar with the PSPP syntax. Data can be entered from the keyboard, imported from spreadsheet applications, or imported from existing files.

There is a spreadsheet type data entry window for the entry and viewing of data and its metadata.

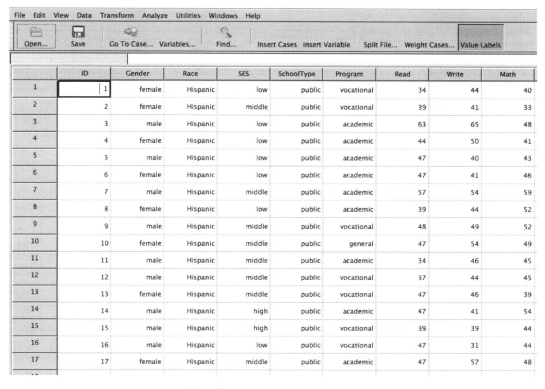

Figure 3: PSPP Data View Window

Drop down menus provide access to all the supported statistical analyses and transformations, in addition to operations such as loading and saving of the data and syntax files. You can use the features via interactive dialog boxes that indicate the options and required parameters of each command. The drop-down menus and dialogs are useful for many analyses. PSPP also supports the syntax mechanism providing a more powerful and flexible means of controlling PSPP. However for the novice researcher, or most researchers for that matter, the Graphic User Interface (GUI) will be a more familiar and comfortable workspace, similar to many other applications that we use everyday.

Output Window

There is also a non-interactive output window. The output window is generated when the user conducts any of the analysis or visualization functions. Each successive operation is appended to the output window. To switch between the data window and the output table window use the Windows menu.

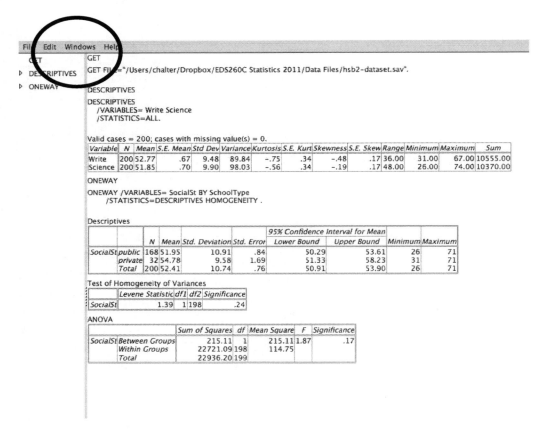

Figure 4: Sample PSPP Output Window

Data Visualization

PSPP can generate plots or graphs to help with the visualization of the data distribution. Among the type of plots that can be displayed are pie charts, normal probability plots and histograms. These complement descriptive statistics and help determine the most appropriate type of analysis for the data. The data selection capabilities of PSPP make it simple to generate plots from a subset of variables or data.

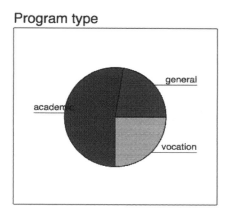

Figure 5: Sample PSPP Pie Chart

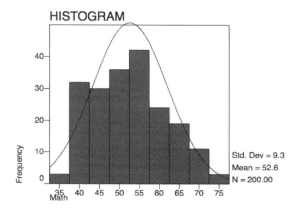

Figure 6: Sample PSPP Histogram

Plots and graphs created by PSPP are formatted in standard file formats such as postscript or PNG, so as to allow easy export and import into reports or other documents. The output tables can be exported as .png, .html, .txt, .jpg, and several other format types.

Chapter 4
Getting Started with PSPP

Preparing the Data and Making Decisions

Now that we have data collected from our study it is time to perform some analysis to address the research questions posed. One of the first choices made deals with entering your data into an application so that you can actually do the analysis. Depending on the kind of data you have collected there are many choices available.

We will focus on using continuous and categorical data sets with the PSPP statistical analysis application.

Creating Your Variable Codebook

Whether you plan to perform data entry into a spreadsheet first or to enter the data directly into PSPP you will need to create a codebook for your data. The codebook is used as a planning tool and a quick reference guide to your data.

There are some questions that must be addressed prior to data entry.

Continuous Data
- How large is your data set?
- Will all the data entries be manually entered into the spreadsheet or PSPP?
- How many decimal places are required for your data?
- How will you "name" the data set for easy reference?
- Are there any outliers in the data set?
- How will you handle outliers?

Categorical Data
- What are the value names for each data item?
- How will you represent each value name with an integer value?
- Is your data nominal or ordinal? How will this guide the decision for selecting values?

Table 6: Data Types and Analysis Methods

Data Type	Possible Analysis Applications
Text data: Interviews, open ended questionnaires, field notes, focus group transcripts, writing samples, etc.	Word processing application (Word or OpenOffice) HyperResearch
Video or Audio recording data	HyperResearch Hypertranscribe Quicktime Transana InqScribe StudioCode
Categorical and Continuous Data	Microsoft Excel OpenOffice Spreadsheets PSPP SPSS SAS

With any categorical data, we begin by converting the labels, such as male/female or private school/public school, into numerical values that can be manipulated in the analysis application.

In the case of our "High School and Beyond" (hsb2.sav) sample dataset the codebook is represented in the table below.

Table 7: CODEBOOK for High School and Beyond Data:

Variable Name	Variable type	Variable Label	Variable Value
gender	Categorical	Gender	0=male 1=female
race	Categorical	Race	1=Hispanic 2=Asian 3=African American

			4=White
ses	Categorical	Socioeconomic status	1=low 2=middle 3=high
schtyp	Categorical	School type	1=public 2=private
prog	Categorical	Program type	1=general 2=academic 3=vocational
read	Continuous	Reading score	
write	Continuous	Writing score	
math	Continuous	Math score	
science	Continuous	Science score	
socst	Continuous	Social Studies score	

Some of the data in our sample set are nominal in nature. There is not any order to the labels and an order should not be implied from the values used. For example, the value for socioeconomic status has been listed "low, middle, and high" with values of "1, 2, and 3" assigned respectively. This does not imply the "low" is first, "middle" is second, and "high" is third. These labels could have been placed in any order and assigned any value.

On the other hand if our sample data had involved grade level or degrees attained, then we might be able to assign values based on an order, so this would represent ordinal data.

Table 8: Sample CODEBOOK for Schooling Data:

Variable Name	Variable type	Variable Label	Variable Value
id	Categorical	Student ID	
gender	Categorical	Gender	0=male 1=female

grade	Categorical	GradeLevel	1=First grade
			2=Second grade
			3=Third grade
			4=Fourth grade
degree	Categorical	Degree Attained	1=Not a High School Graduate
			2=High School Diploma
			3=Bachelors degree
			4=Graduate degree

Creating Variable/Data Names in PSPP

When PSPP is launched, the user is presented with a blank table. At the bottom of the table there are two choices for the view; data view and variable view. **Data View** allows you enter data or to see the data that has previously been entered. **Variable View** allows you to define your variables for the data.

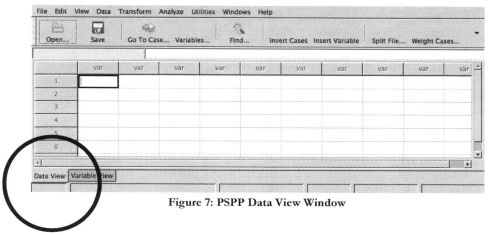

Figure 7: PSPP Data View Window

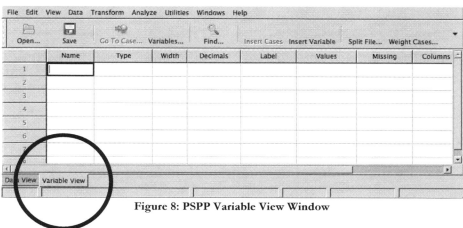

Figure 8: PSPP Variable View Window

Before data can be entered into PSPP you must define your variables. This is where your data codebook is useful since we have already defined the types of data and the values that will be needed for our analysis.

- But what order should the variables be entered?
- How will you group the values so that they make sense and allow you to use them more efficiently?

In the PSPP environment, the **variable window** presents each variable in a row. Each column will define a specific aspect of that variable, such as the name of the variable, the data type for the variable (typically deciding if it is a string/name or numerical), the width or amount of numbers to show, the decimal places required, etc.

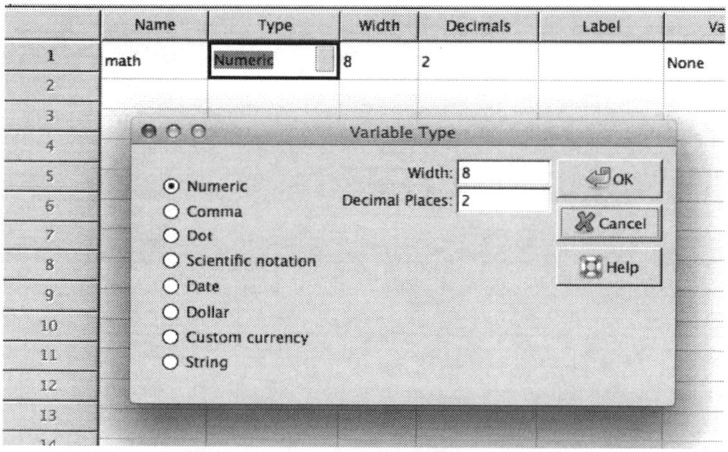

Figure 9: Variable Type Dialogue Box

Once a variable name has been entered the other columns are activated so that you can define that variable more completely.

The **data view window** then displays each variable or data type as a column and each row will be a case. The case is the level of fine grain detail available for the analysis. In the hsb2 data set each case represents a single participant in the study.

Defining Continuous Data

In defining continuous data, enter the short name of your variable, such as math (to represent a math score). For the data type, click on the popup window icon (shown as a rectangle in the cell) and select "numeric" for a continuous data entry. Within the popup box you can also select the maximum length of the value and the decimal places required.

Once the variable has been defined, you can change or edit these values by clicking in the cell to activate the selection arrows. Click on the up or down arrows to increase or decrease the value.

File	Edit	View	Data	Transform	Analyze	Utilities	Windows	Help		
		Open...		Save	Go To Case...	Variables...		Find...	Insert Cases	Ins
	Name		Type		Width	Decimals		Label		
1	math		Numeric		8	2				
2										
3										
4										
5										
6										
7										
8										

Figure 10: Variable View Defining Decimal Places

Defining Categorical Data

When a categorical value is entered within PSPP, the "value" must also be defined. The value is the numerical integer that will be used to represent the data in PSPP and allow for the application to perform statistical analysis with that data.

When the codebook was created we decided beforehand the values that would be assigned for each categorical data type. As shown previously for continuous data entry, once the variable name has been entered the other cells will become active so that they can be defined as well. Be sure to select "string" from the "variable type" option in the popup menu. **String** will define the data as categorical while **Numeric** designates the data as continuous.

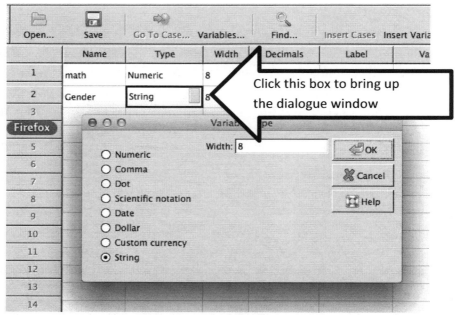

Figure 11: Dialogue Box to Define the Variable Type

To define the values to be used for our categorical data, click the rectangle in the "Value" cell to show the popup menu (see the figure below). In this menu enter the value name, such as male/female, the then the value to be assigned to each name.

The value names must be entered one at a time and the "+Add" button clicked. Once all the values are entered you can click "OK" to close the menu. Be sure to enter the correct numerical representation into the "Value" box and the label that is to be used in the "Value label" box.

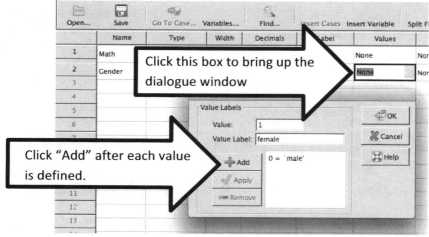

Figure 12: Dialogue Box to Define Values

Entering Data Directly into PSPP

The data can be entered directly into PSPP in the **Data View** screen. Each row will be one of the cases for which you have collected data. When entering categorical data be sure to enter the **values** that you have defined in the codebook and not the name or label for the data. After the data has been entered use the "Value Label" button along the top menu bar to switch the view between variable values and variable labels. This will allow you to switch between the numeric values of your data and the labels describing that data, see the figures below.

This is an important note worth repeating; when entering categorical values directly into PSPP, you must enter the numerical value and **NOT** the name or the label used. Having your data codebook handy will help with data entry.

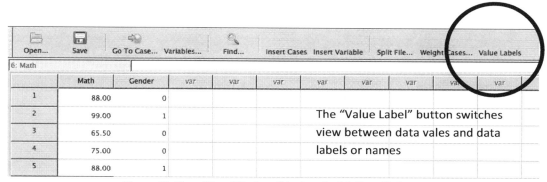

Figure 13: Data View Window Displayed with Data Values

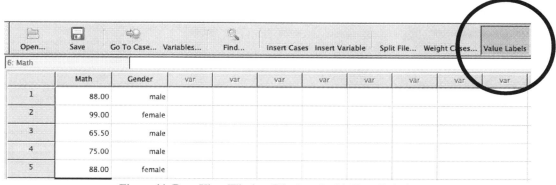

Figure 14: Data View Window Displayed with Data Labels

Importing Data File into PSPP (.sav files)

The PSPP statistical application is able to natively use and save .sav file formats. This means that files created within SPSS, or any other compatible application can be easily opened with PSPP without having to convert the file.

Using File > Open from the top menu, select the .sav data file from your computer.

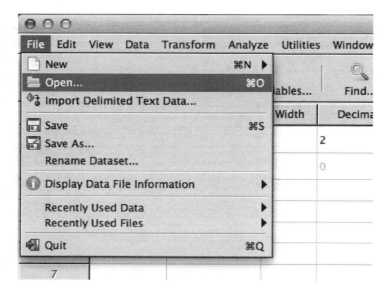

Figure 15: PSPP Open Command

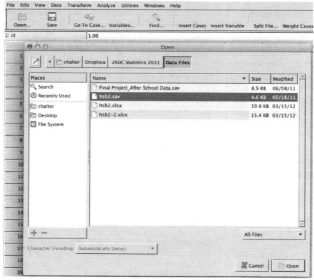

Figure 16: PSPP Open Dialogue Box

The file will open with the variable names and data.

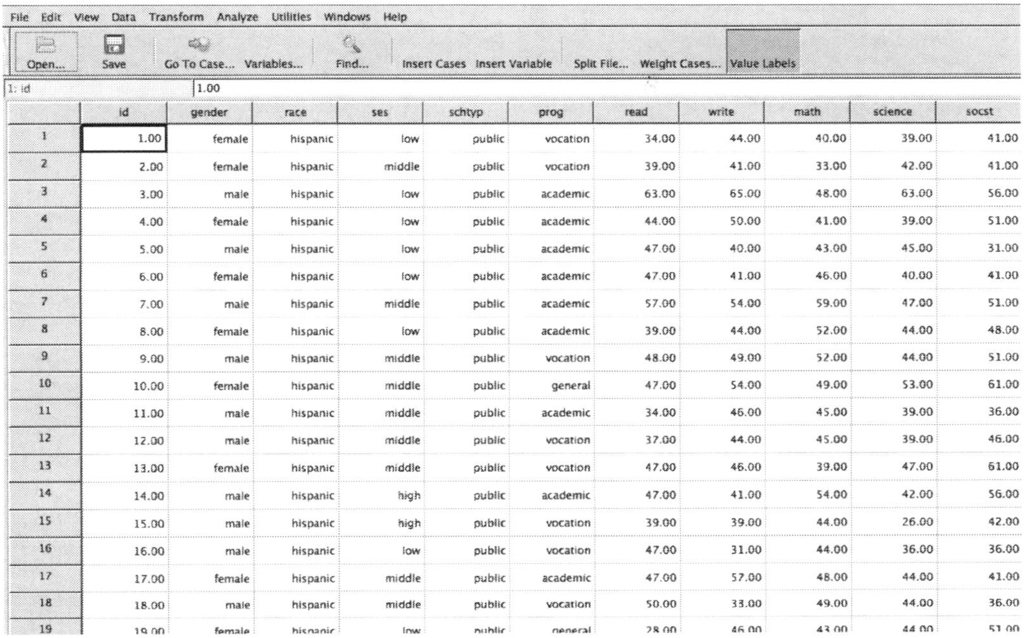

	id	gender	race	ses	schtyp	prog	read	write	math	science	socst
1	1.00	female	hispanic	low	public	vocation	34.00	44.00	40.00	39.00	41.00
2	2.00	female	hispanic	middle	public	vocation	39.00	41.00	33.00	42.00	41.00
3	3.00	male	hispanic	low	public	academic	63.00	65.00	48.00	63.00	56.00
4	4.00	female	hispanic	low	public	academic	44.00	50.00	41.00	39.00	51.00
5	5.00	male	hispanic	low	public	academic	47.00	40.00	43.00	45.00	31.00
6	6.00	female	hispanic	low	public	academic	47.00	41.00	46.00	40.00	41.00
7	7.00	male	hispanic	middle	public	academic	57.00	54.00	59.00	47.00	51.00
8	8.00	female	hispanic	low	public	academic	39.00	44.00	52.00	44.00	48.00
9	9.00	male	hispanic	middle	public	vocation	48.00	49.00	52.00	44.00	51.00
10	10.00	female	hispanic	middle	public	general	47.00	54.00	49.00	53.00	61.00
11	11.00	male	hispanic	middle	public	academic	34.00	46.00	45.00	39.00	36.00
12	12.00	male	hispanic	middle	public	vocation	37.00	44.00	45.00	39.00	46.00
13	13.00	female	hispanic	middle	public	vocation	47.00	46.00	39.00	47.00	61.00
14	14.00	male	hispanic	high	public	academic	47.00	41.00	54.00	42.00	56.00
15	15.00	male	hispanic	high	public	vocation	39.00	39.00	44.00	26.00	42.00
16	16.00	male	hispanic	low	public	vocation	47.00	31.00	44.00	36.00	36.00
17	17.00	female	hispanic	middle	public	academic	47.00	57.00	48.00	44.00	41.00
18	18.00	male	hispanic	middle	public	vocation	50.00	33.00	49.00	44.00	36.00
19	19.00	female	hispanic	low	public	general	28.00	46.00	43.00	44.00	51.00

Figure 17: PSPP with Imported Data

PSPP can also open ".txt" files that contain delimited text, ".sps" syntax files that are also created by SPSS, and ".por" which is a SPSS portability file to exchange data.

Importing Data Files into PSPP from a Spreadsheet (.cvs files)

You may find that entering your data into a spreadsheet has some advantages for you over entering directly into the PSPP table. It may also be the case that your data is already contained in a spreadsheet. PSPP is able to import this data, however it cannot import directly from the spreadsheet file. PSPP can only import UTF-8 (8-bit Unicode Transformational Format) text data.

Just as a warning, the next several sentences may make your eyes glaze over as it will get a bit technical. But bear with me, it will make sense in a moment.

Most spreadsheet applications can export your data as simple ASCII text files. These are simple formats that can be opened by many different application programs. The most common format is the ".cvs" delimited text file, which indicates that the data is separated by commas. While some programs use the UTF-8 format to export the text files others use the UTF-16 (16-bit Unicode Transformational Format) to encode and export the data. PSPP can only import files encoded in UTF-8.

In the world of spreadsheets perhaps the two most commonly used are Microsoft Excel, using both the UTF-16 and UTF-8 format, and OpenOffice Spreadsheets using the UTF-8 format. As you may have guessed, your data can be entered into either MS Excel or OpenOffice Spreadsheets but before it can be imported into PSPP, the file must be exported as a ".cvs" file with UTF-8 encoding.

Either spreadsheet application can be used and OpenOffice can use the file whether it is an OpenOffice file (.ods) or a MS Excel file (.xls or .xlsx).

Setting Up the Spreadsheet

Getting the spreadsheet setup and the data entered is a simple process. There are a few key points to keep in mind:

- In the spreadsheet, the columns contain each variable or data type and the rows represent each case in the study. This is similar to the way PSPP displays the data.
- The first row of the spreadsheet will be the variable names with row 2 containing the first data set. Variable names should be short. Variable names must be less than 64 characters long.
- Categorical data must be entered as its numerical value and not the name. The codebook you created will come in handy for this process.
- Enter all the data.

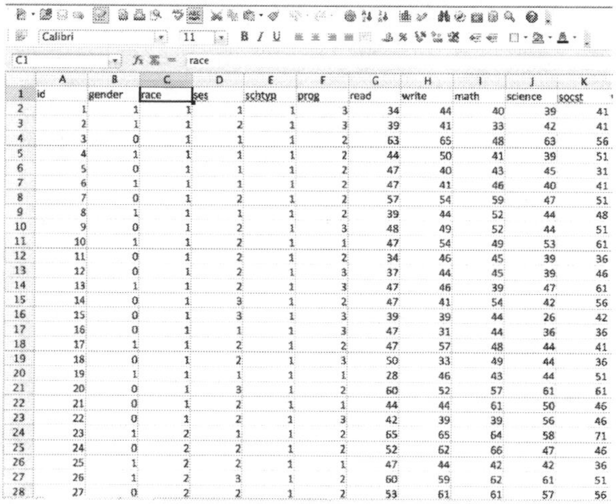

	A	B	C	D	E	F	G	H	I	J	K
1	id	gender	race	ses	schtyp	prog	read	write	math	science	socst
2	1	1	1	1	1	3	34	44	40	39	41
3	2	1	1	2	1	3	39	41	33	42	41
4	3	0	1	1	1	2	63	65	48	63	56
5	4	1	1	1	1	2	44	50	41	39	51
6	5	0	1	1	1	2	47	40	43	45	31
7	6	1	1	1	1	2	47	41	46	40	41
8	7	0	1	2	1	2	57	54	59	47	51
9	8	1	1	1	1	2	39	44	52	44	48
10	9	0	1	2	1	3	48	49	52	44	51
11	10	1	1	2	1	1	47	54	49	53	61
12	11	0	1	2	1	2	34	46	45	39	36
13	12	0	1	2	1	3	37	44	45	39	46
14	13	1	1	2	1	3	47	46	39	47	61
15	14	0	1	3	1	2	47	41	54	42	56
16	15	0	1	3	1	3	39	39	44	26	42
17	16	0	1	1	1	3	47	31	44	36	36
18	17	1	1	2	1	2	47	57	48	44	41
19	18	0	1	2	1	3	50	33	49	44	36
20	19	1	1	1	1	1	28	46	43	44	51
21	20	0	1	3	1	2	60	52	57	61	61
22	21	0	1	2	1	1	44	44	61	50	46
23	22	0	1	2	1	3	42	39	39	56	46
24	23	1	2	1	1	2	65	65	64	58	71
25	24	0	2	2	1	2	52	62	66	47	46
26	25	1	2	2	1	1	47	44	42	42	36
27	26	1	2	3	1	2	60	59	62	61	51
28	27	0	2	2	1	2	53	61	61	57	56

Figure 18: OpenOffice Spreadsheet with data labels shown as numerical values vice names

Saving the File Using OpenOffice

The next step to prepare this data file to import into PSPP is to save the file as a ".cvs" UTF-8 text file. Use the menu at the top of the screen to select File > Save As.

From the pull down menu select the Text (.cvs) format. If a warning screen comes up click on "Keep Current Format", and be sure to select the UTF-8 character set.

Again, in order to save the file in the proper format, follow these steps;

1. Select the file type to be "Text CVS (.cvs)" in the dialogue box and click "Save".

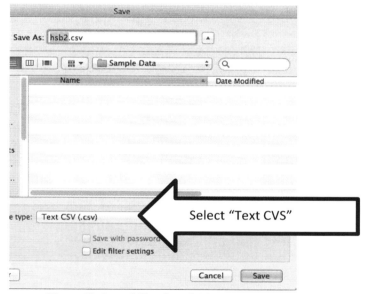

Figure 19: OpenOffice Save Dialogue Box

2. Another dialogue box will come up. Click "Keep Current Format"

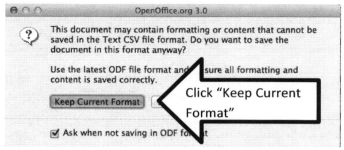

Figure 20: Keep Current Format window

3. From the Character Set pull down menu, select "Unicode (UTF-8).

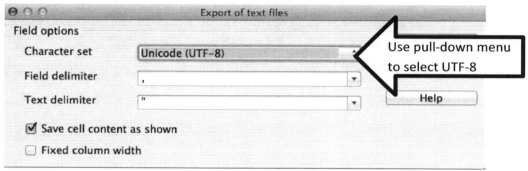

Figure 21: OpenOffice Character Set Dialogue Box

Saving the File Using Excel

The spreadsheet can also be saved and imported by PSPP using Excel. The Apple OS version of Excel may not automatically output the .cvs delimited file in the UTF-8 format. When using Excel for Windows simply use the "Save As" function to create the text file as Comma Separated (.cvs). When using the Apple OS version of Excel, use the "Save As" function and save your file as the "Windows Comma Separated" (.cvs) format, as shown the figure below.

Figure 22: Excel Save As Menu

Importing Data Into PSPP

Now we are ready to import the spreadsheet data into PSPP. From the file menu at the top of the window select File > Import Delimited Text. A dialogue box will appear for you to select the file to import into PSPP.

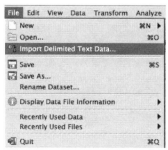

Figure 23: PSPP Import

Once the file begins to import, there will be several popup windows to help format the data so that PSPP can use it. In the first screen be sure that "All Cases" is selected.

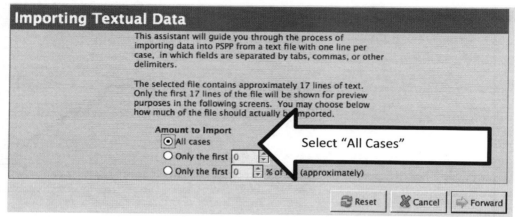

Figure 24: PSPP Importing Data

Since we are using row 1 for the variable names, on the next popup screen click on the line 2 as shown in the figure below and click the box at the bottom of the screen to indicate that the first row contains variable names.

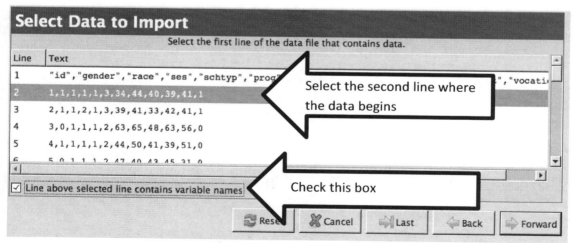

Figure 25: PSPP Select Data to Import

Verify that "Comma" is selected as the character separator.

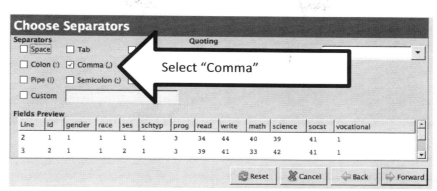

Figure 26: PSPP Separators Selection

The next step will require you to verify the data types. The default setting in PSPP is to make every variable a numeric value. For all the categorical data we must override this setting and give the variable a variable label and value. Again, this is where we will use the codebook to match numeric values to each label used for the categorical data. The next few steps will let PSPP know what labels to give to those numeric categorical values.

Click on the variable type setting to activate the dialog box. Click "String" to identify the data type as categorical.

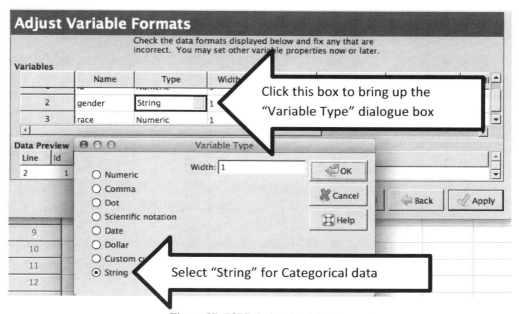

Figure 27: PSPP Adjust Variable Format

Now we must input all the labels and values to be associated with those names. This is another good time to refer to your data codebook. Click on the "Values" cell to activate the dialog box.

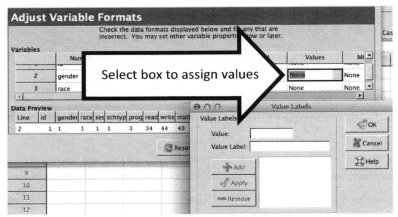

Figure 28: Assigning Values in PSPP

Using your data codebook as a reference, enter each variable value and the value label. Be sure to use the "+Add" button to add the value and name, clicking "OK" when completed. Use your codebook to enter the data's numeric value in the "Value" box and the label or name of the data in the "Value Label" box.

In the example we have entered a value of "0" for the label "males" and a value of "1" for the label "females". After each value and label is entered click the "Add" button to create the label. This will allow you to view the category names instead of the assigned numerical values.

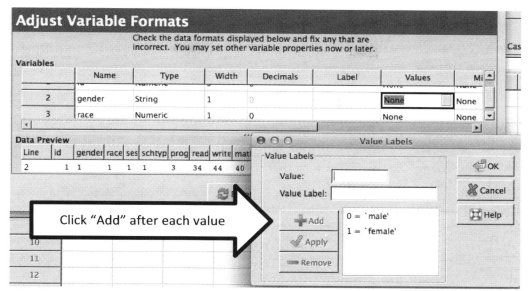

Figure 29: Value Label Box

The above steps must be completed for each line of categorical data in your dataset.

After all the categorical lines of data gave been updated, click "Apply" and PSPP will import the data set.

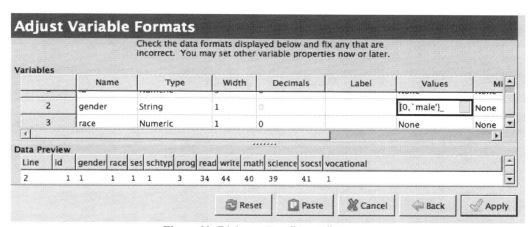

Figure 30: Dialogue Box "Apply" Button

The imported data will appear in the data view window of PSPP. To switch between the label names and the label values use the "Value Label" button at the top of the screen.

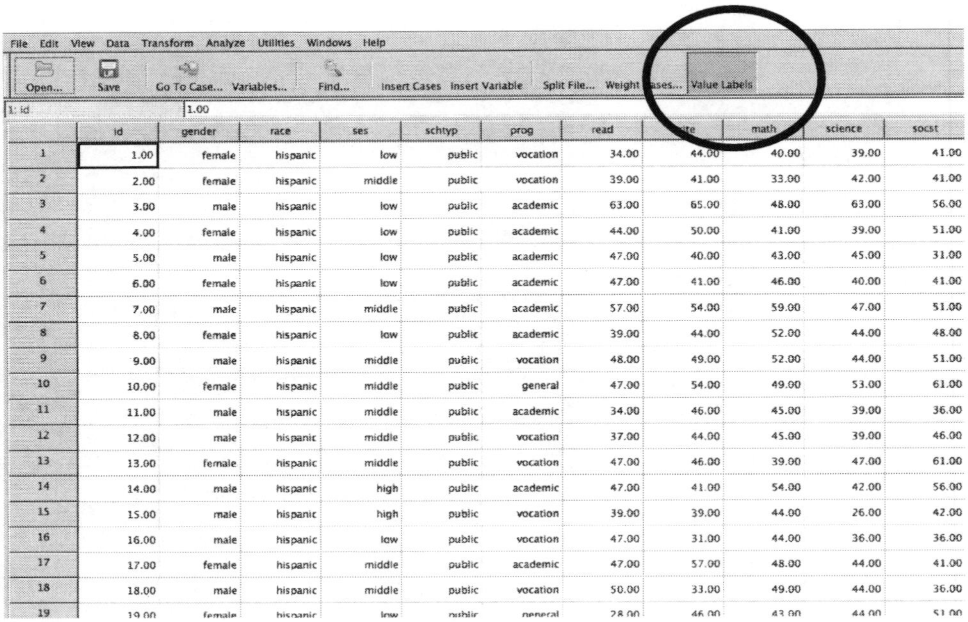

Figure 31: Completed Import Process

Chapter 5
Descriptive Statistics

What are descriptive statistics?

Descriptive statistics is a method to characterize the data in order to make decisions about the nature, tendencies, and appropriate inferential statistics that can be used to analyze the data. In descriptive statistics we look at various measures such as mean, median, mode, and standard deviations. These measures provide us with a way to represent large data sets.

Creating Descriptive Statistics in PSPP for Categorical Data

1. Categorical data is best described by exploring the frequencies within the data. The frequencies will display the percentages of each category within the data set.

2. Use the PSPP menu Analyze > Descriptive Statistics > Frequencies

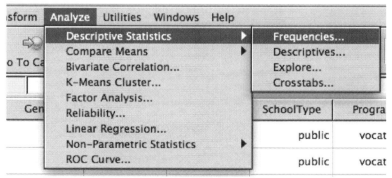

Figure 32: PSPP Descriptive Statistics Frequencies Menu

3. From the dialogue box select the categorical data needed and move them into the

"Variable(s)" window. None of the "Statistics" are required for this sort of data. Click "OK".

In order to select the variables, click and highlight the variable, such as gender, SES, etc., from the window on the left side of the dialogue window and click the arrow to move it into the "Variable(s)" window. More than one variable can be entered into the Variables window.

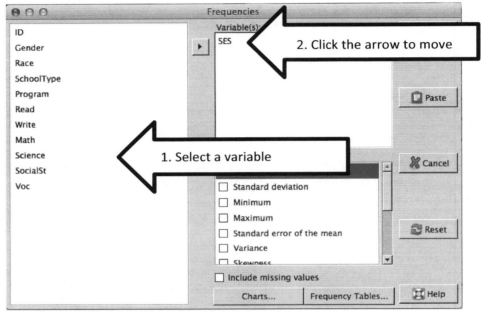

Figure 33: Frequencies Selection Window

4. The Output window will display a frequencies and percentages table for the selected categorical data.

```
FREQUENCIES
    /VARIABLES= SES
    /FORMAT=AVALUE TABLE
    /STATISTICS=NONE.
```

SES

Value Label	Value	Frequency	Percent	Valid Percent	Cum Percent
low	1	47	23.50	23.50	23.50
middle	2	95	47.50	47.50	71.00
high	3	58	29.00	29.00	100.00
	Total	200	100.0	100.0	

Figure 34: Frequencies Output Table

Creating Visual Representations for Categorical Data

1. Visual representations such as **pie charts** and **bar graphs** can be a valuable tool in analyzing a data set. The chart can display features of the data set that may not be as evident in the numerical representation. For categorical data, pie charts may be the most useful visualization.

2. Creating either type of chart within PSPP is accomplished by using the menu Analyze > Descriptive Statistics > Frequencies.

3. In the dialogue box click on the "Charts" button.

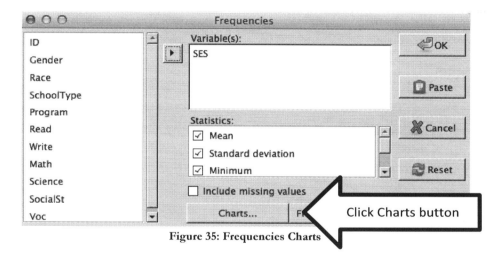

Figure 35: Frequencies Charts

4. In the Charts dialogue box select the pie chart checkbox for categorical data.

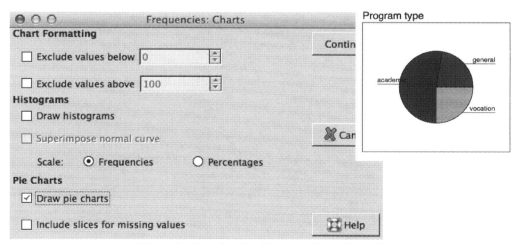

Figure 36: Creating Pie Charts and Sample Pie Chart

Creating Descriptive Statistics in PSPP for Continuous Data

1. Continuous data lends itself to descriptive statistics that focus on variation and measures of central tendency. Mean, median, mode, range, maximum and minimum values, standard deviation, etc. can provide valuable information about the continuous data.

2. Using the PSPP menu select Analyze > Descriptive Statistics > Descriptives

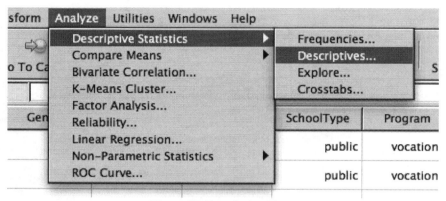

Figure 37: Descriptive Menu

3. In the dialogue box select the checkboxes for the descriptive statistics to be displayed in the output table. In this example we have selected mean, median, minimum, maximum, range, standard deviation, and variance.

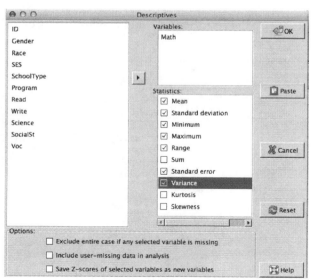

Figure 38: Descriptive Statistics

4. In the output window the descriptive statistics table is generated.

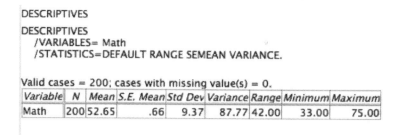

DESCRIPTIVES
DESCRIPTIVES
    /VARIABLES= Math
    /STATISTICS=DEFAULT RANGE SEMEAN VARIANCE.

Valid cases = 200; cases with missing value(s) = 0.

Variable	N	Mean	S.E. Mean	Std Dev	Variance	Range	Minimum	Maximum
Math	200	52.65	.66	9.37	87.77	42.00	33.00	75.00

Figure 39: Descriptives Output Table

Creating Visual Representations for Continuous Data

1. Visual representations such as bar charts, also called **histograms**, can be a valuable tool used in analyzing a continuous data set. The chart can display features of the data set that may not be as evident otherwise.

2. Creating a histogram chart within PSPP is accomplished by using the menu Analyze > Descriptive Statistics > Frequencies

3. In the dialogue box click on the "Charts" button after the data has been entered into the Variables window.

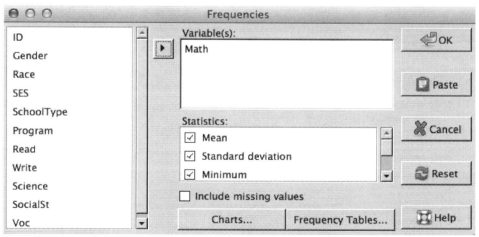

Figure 40: Frequencies Window

4. In the Charts dialogue box select the histogram chart. A histogram works best for displaying continuous data. By selecting "Superimpose normal curve" you will be able to inspect your data for a normal distribution.

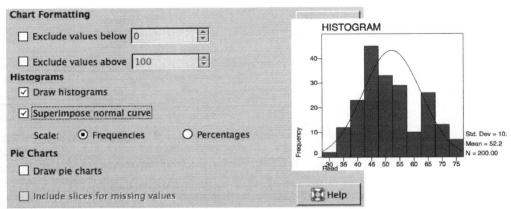

Figure 41: Chart Dialogue Box with Sample Histogram

Interpreting Output Tables: Descriptives

In this example we have a sample descriptive output table for both the Reading Test scores and the Math Test scores from our data set. The table was created by using the Analyze > Descriptive Statistics > Frequencies menu. Both Math and Reading scores were moved to the Variable(s) window and in the charts menu the histogram with superimpose normal curve checkbox was selected. Each variable selected will be shown in a row of the output table.

```
DESCRIPTIVES
  /VARIABLES= Math Read
  /STATISTICS=DEFAULT RANGE VARIANCE KURTOSIS SKEWNESS.
```

Valid cases = 200; cases with missing value(s) = 0.

Variable	N	Mean	Std Dev	Variance	Kurtosis	S.E. Kurt	Skewness	S.E. Skew	Range	Minimum	Maximum
Math	200	52.65	9.37	87.77	-.65	.34	.29	.17	42.00	33.00	75.00
Read	200	52.23	10.25	105.12	-.62	.34	.20	.17	48.00	28.00	76.00

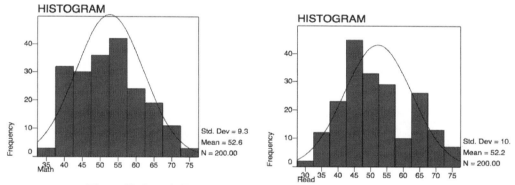

Figure 42: Sample Frequencies output table for math & reading scores

1. The "Mean" will give us the average score in the data. This output table shows us the mean score for both the math and reading test. We also find that the means of the two test scores are almost the same.

2. The "Minimum" and "Maximum" columns give the lowest and highest score for each test. Here we notice that the maximum was about the same on each test and that the Reading test had a slightly lower minimum score.

3. "Standard Deviation" (Std Dev column) gives a measure of the variation in our test scores from the mean. The scores can be described as 1 standard deviation from the mean, or 2 standard deviations from the mean, or 3 standard deviations from the mean. The standard deviations follow the 68-95-99 rule in statistics, in that 68% of the data falls within the first standard deviation, 95% of the data falls within the second standard deviation, and 99% of the data falls within the third standard deviation.

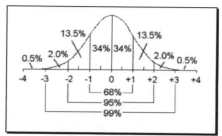

Figure 43: Standard Deviation Diagram

In reviewing the math and reading scores, the standard deviation for the math scores is smaller than the standard deviation for the reading scores, or there is less variance in the math scores, which is also evident by comparing the value in our "Variance" column of the output table.

We would find that 68% of the math scores are between 43.28 and 62.02. In comparison, 68% of the reading scores are between 41.98 and 62.48.

4. **Kurtosis** describes the "peakness" of the data. A kurtosis value of zero represents data that resembles a normally distributed data set. Positive values represent data with a **leptokurtic** distribution, or very high peaks, and negative values represent data with a **platykurtic** distribution, or one that is more flat. In this example we find that both data sets have a slight negative Kurtosis indicating some "flatness" to the histogram.

5. **Skewness** gives us information about the distribution of data from the mean. A skewness value of zero would have data evenly distributed and balanced around the mean. A positive skewness value indicates data weighted more heavily to the right of the mean and a negative skewness value indicates data weighted to the left of the mean. In this example both sets of scores have a slight positive skewness value.

6. A histogram of the data can also reveal important features about the scores prior to conducting any inferential analysis.

Chapter 6
Box & Whisker Plots Using OpenOffice Spreadsheets

In descriptive statistics one of the most useful visualizations is the box plot, or sometimes referred to as a Box & Whisker Plot. PSPP does not produce box plots of your data. However I think that they are so useful and interesting that we will explore creating them here.

1. A Box Plot or Box & Whisker Plot can provide valuable visual information about continuous data. A box plot sorts the data into quartiles and can easily display any outliers within the data set.

The main feature of a **box & whisker plot** is that the data is represented in quartiles. Each quartile, or section of the plot, represents 25% of the data points. So if we had a data set of test scores with 80 students, then 20 student scores would be in the first quartile, 20 scores in the second quartile, 20 scores in the third quartile, and 20 scores in the fourth quartile.

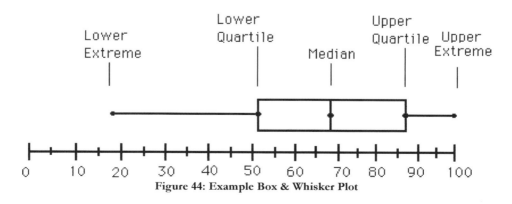

Figure 44: Example Box & Whisker Plot

2. PSPP currently does not create box plots, although this may change with future updates to the application. The open source application OpenOffice can create a box plot, as can most other spreadsheet applications.

3. The first step to creating a **box plot** in OpenOffice is to calculate the 5 measures for your data; minimum value, first quartile, median, third quartile, and maximum value. In your spreadsheet create a worksheet with the continuous data. In this example we have math test scores. Create a place for the 5 value measures. We will need to find the **values** for these measures from the data.

E2		▼	f_x Σ =		
	A	**B**	**C**	**D**	**E**
1	Math Scores			Values	Plot Points
2	44		Min.		
3	48		Q1		
4	49		Median		
5	39		Q3		
6	54		Max.		
7	44				
8	39				
9	57				

Figure 45: Sample Spreadsheet Set-up

4. Select the cell that will contain your minimum score value. Click the function menu and select "MIN". Click "Next" then select the scores to be used to calculate the minimum value. You can select the cells to include in the function by entering the cell range or by clicking and dragging across all the cells to include in the function. Then click "OK".

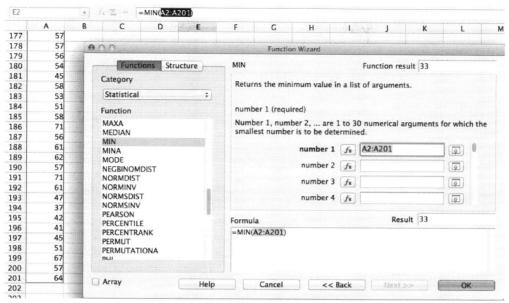

Figure 46: Function Wizard Window for MIN

5. The value cell will now contain the minimum score from the selected data.

	A	B	C	D	E
1	Math Scores			Values	Plot Points
2	44		Min.	33	
3	48		Q1		
4	49		Median		
5	39		Q3		
6	54		Max.		
7	44				
8	39				
9	57				

Figure 47: OpenOffice Spreadsheet Cells

6. Select the cell that will contain your maximum score value. Click the function menu and select "MAX". Click "Next" then select the scores to be used to calculate the maximum value. You can select the cells to include in the function by entering the cell range, by copying and pasting the values from the previous function, or by clicking and dragging across all the cells to include in the function. Then click "OK".

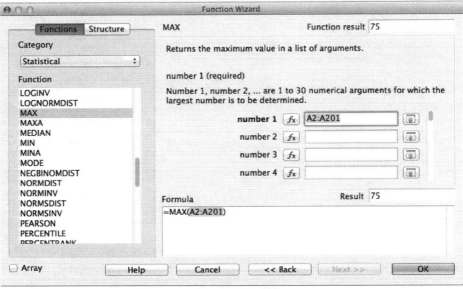

Figure 48: Function Wizard Window for MAX

7. Select the cell that will contain your median score value. Click the function menu and select "MEDIAN". Click "Next" then select the scores to be used to calculate the median value. You can select the cells to include in the function by entering the cell range, by copying and pasting the values from the previous function, or by clicking and dragging across all the cells to include in the function. Then click "OK".

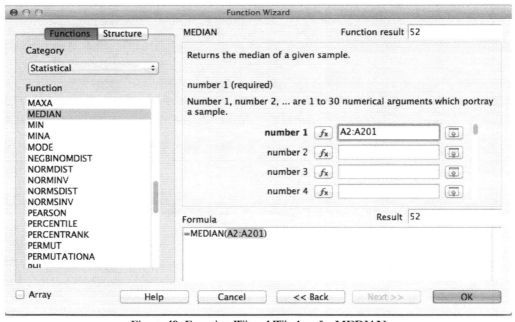

Figure 49: Function Wizard Window for MEDIAN

8. Calculate the first quartile with the QUARTILE function. In the dialogue box select the data to be used in the calculation. Enter a "1" in the Type box to calculate the first quartile. You can select the cells to include in the function by entering the cell range, by copying and pasting the values from the previous function, or by clicking and dragging across all the cells to include in the function. Then click "OK".

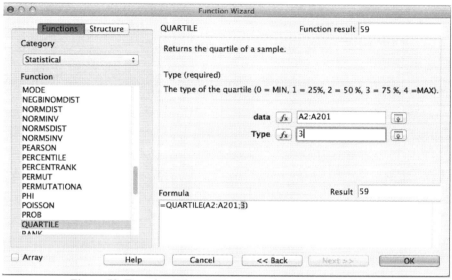

Figure 50: Function Wizard Window for THIRD QUARTILE

9. Calculate the third quartile with the QUARTILE function. In the dialogue box select the data to be used in the calculation. Enter a "3" in the Type box to calculate the third quartile. You can select the cells to include in the function by entering the cell range, by copying and pasting the values from the previous function, or by clicking and dragging across all the cells to include in the function. Then click "OK".

10. Once the box plot values have been calculated we will create the plot values that will be used to create the graph.

	A	B	C	D	E
1	Math Scores			Values	Plot Points
2	44		Min.	33	
3	48		Q1	45	
4	49		Median	52	
5	39		Q3	59	
6	54		Max.	75	
7	44				
8	39				
9	57				

Figure 51: Plot Points Prior to Calculations

11. The "Plot Points" are needed to create the box plot. The Minimum Plot Point is the same as the calculated minimum Value ("33" in the example above). The Q1 Plot Point is Q1 value minus the Minimum value (Q1 – MIN). The median plot point is the median value minus the Q1 value (MEDIAN – Q1), the Q3 plot value is the Q3 value minus the median value (Q3 – MEDIAN), and the maximum plot point is the maximum value minus the Q3 value (MAX – Q3).

	A	B	C	D	E
1	Math Scores			Values	Plot Points
2	44		Min.	33	33
3	48		Q1	45	12
4	49		Median	52	7
5	39		Q3	59	7
6	54		Max.	75	16
7	44				
8	39				
9	57				

Figure 52: Plot points After Calculations

12. To create the graph select the Plot Point numbers. Click the Chart Wizard and select the "Stacked Bar Graph" in the Chart Type step, click Next, and in the Data Range step select "Data Series in Rows".

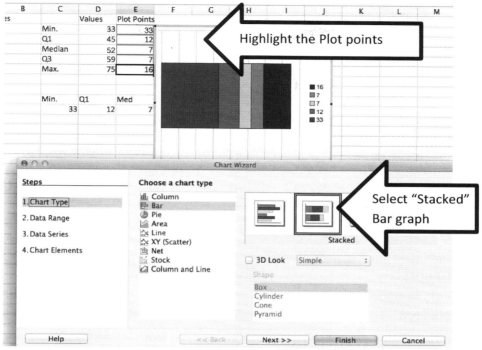

Figure 53: Chart Wizard Bar Graphs

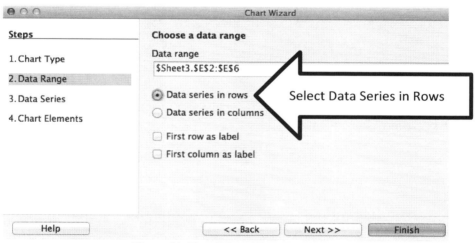

Figure 54: Chart Wizard Data Range

13. This process will create a **stacked bar graph** that extends from zero to the maximum value. Now we must format the bars to look like a box plot. Below is a sample of the bar graph with the sections labeled as A, B, C, D, & E. We will format these sections to create a box plot.

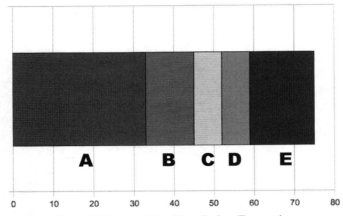

Figure 55: Stacked Bar Chart Before Formatting

14. Right-Click (or Control-Click) the two sections on the far left to view the formatting dialogue window for the data series, labeled as sections "A" and "B" above. In our example this is the area from 0 to 33 and 33 to 45. Set the area transparency and the border transparency to 100%. Select the same settings for the area to the far right of the graph, labeled section "E". Only sections "C" and "D" will remain visible.

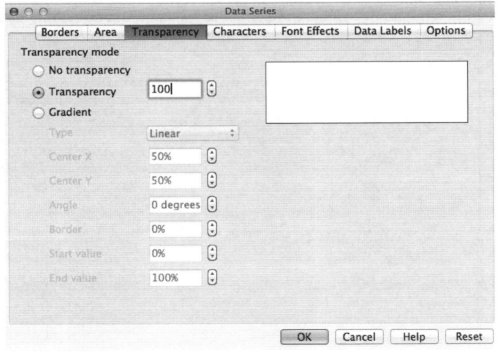

Figure 56: Chart Wizard Transparency Settings

15. Right-click (or Control-Click) the transparent section to the left of the lower visible bar, labeled section "B". Select "Insert Y-Error Bars" and set this to Percentage, 100%, and Negative.

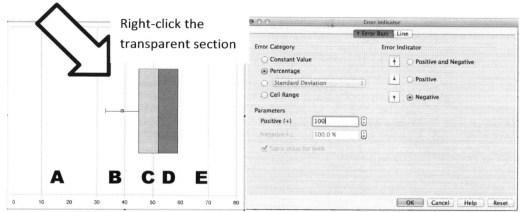

Figure 57: Chart Wizard Negative Error Bars

16. Right-click (or Control-Click) the visible bar to the right, labeled as section "D". Select "Insert Y-Error Bars" and set this to Percentage, 100%, and Positive.

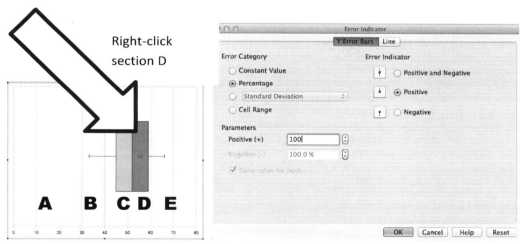

Figure 58: Chart Wizard Positive Error Bars

17. The scale of the chart can be adjusted so that the Box Plot fits the chart area. Select the scale on the chart and insert values that fit. Click on the graph's scale to view the settings dialogue window. Uncheck automatic for the minimum and maximum for the axis scale. Enter your values for the new minimum and maximum, shown as "30" and "70" in the figure below.

Christopher P. Halter

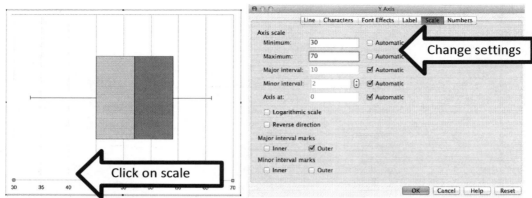

Figure 59; Chart Wizard Scale Setting

18. The Box & Whisker Plot is complete.

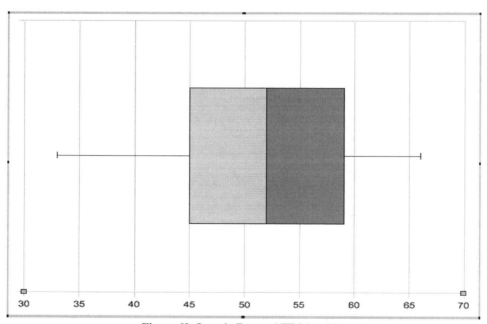

Figure 60: Sample Box and Whisker Plot

Chapter 7
Relationship Analysis with Chi-Square

Chi-Square Analysis (Categorical Differences)

The Chi Square (or Crosstabs) analysis method is used to find differences between categorical data items. The PSPP output table will produce a Chi Square value that can then be compared to a Chi Square table of critical values. If the calculated value is greater than the critical value then the differences are statistically significant.

Chi Square Critical values					
	p value				
df	**0.20**	**0.10**	**0.05**	**0.01**	**0.001**
1	1.64	2.71	3.84	6.63	10.83
2	3.22	4.61	5.99	9.21	13.82
3	4.64	6.25	7.81	11.34	16.27
4	5.59	7.78	9.49	13.23	18.47
5	7.29	9.24	11.07	15.09	20.51
6	8.56	10.64	12.53	16.81	22.46
7	5.80	12.02	14.07	18.48	24.32
8	11.03	13.36	15.51	20.09	26.12
9	12.24	14.68	16.92	21.67	27.83

Figure 61: Chi Square Table of Critical Values

Using the Chi-Square Distribution Table

- The first row of numbers shown in the figure above indicates the confidence level used by the researcher. A confidence interval of 0.05 is used most often in social science and educational research. This represents a 95% confidence level.
- Use the degrees of freedom (df) from the PSPP output table on the corresponding df row in the critical values table. Read the values across that row until you find the critical value in the column representing your confidence level, which will be 0.05 in most cases.
- Compare the calculated Chi Square value with the critical value in the table.
- If the calculated Chi Square value from the PSPP output table is greater than the critical value, then the difference is significant.

Using the Chi-Square Function in PSPP

1. Using the menu, select Analyze>Descriptive Statistics>Crosstabs

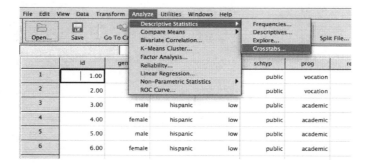

Figure 62: PSPP Chi Square (Crosstabs) Function

2. In the dialog box select one of the categorical variables for the row and another categorical variable for the column. Using the "Statistics" button in the dialogue window the Chi square test should be selected.

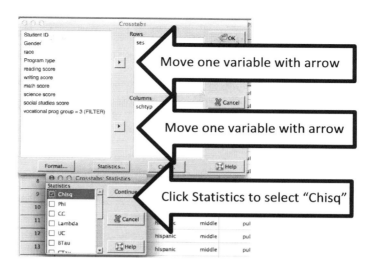

Figure 63: Chi Square Selection Window

3. In the output window review the "Chi-Square tests" output table and find the Pearson Chi Square value. Compare this value with the value in the table of critical values. Be sure to use the correct degrees of freedom and confidence level for your comparison to the critical value.

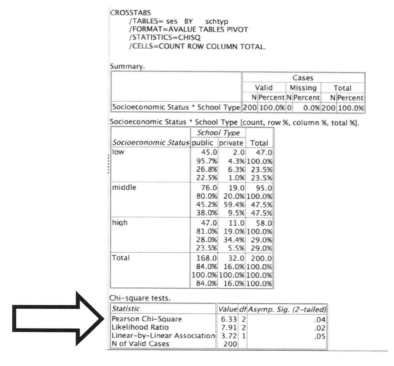

Figure 64: Chi Square Output Table

4. If the calculated chi square value is greater than the critical value from the distribution table, then the difference between the variables is statistically significant.

We can also find the calculated p-value for the Chi Square test in the "Chi-square tests" output table in the column labeled "Asymp. Sig. (2-tailed)". This column displays the calculated two-tailed p-value for the test. In our example above the calculated p-value is 0.04, which is less than our confidence level of 0.05 (but not by much).

It should be noted that the PSPP output tables will only show calculated p-values to two decimal places. Therefore any calculated values that appear as ".00" should be reported as "p < 0.01".

Interpreting Output Tables: Chi Square

In this example we have two Chi Square output tables, also called Crosstabs. The output table on the left is determining if there are differences in Program Type enrollment (Academic, General, and Vocational) based on Race. The output table on the right is determining if there are differences in Program Type enrollment based on socioeconomic status or SES levels (low, middle, and high).

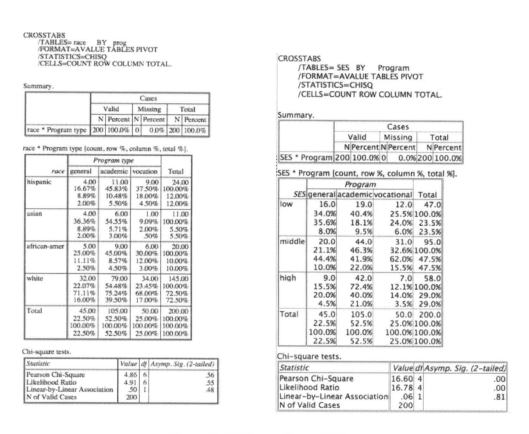

Figure 65: Chi Square Output Tables

1. In examining the Chi Square output table we are interested in the "Chi-square tests" table. The values we use can be found in the first row of the table labeled "Pearson Chi-Square".

2. The second and third columns of the Chi-square tests output table contain the Chi square value and the degrees of freedom (df). The Chi square value along with the degrees of freedom is compared to the critical value on a table of Chi square statistics (see Chi Square Critical Values Table in the appendix). If the Chi square

value is greater than the table's critical value for the specific degrees of freedom, then the difference is significant. If the value is less than the critical value then the difference is not significant.

In the table representing the Race by Program results, we find that the calculated value of 4.86 (df 6) is not greater than the critical value of 12.53 (see Chi square critical values in Appendix), so the differences are not significant. We can also determine that this result is not significant by the p value of p= 0.56, as shown in the "Asymp. Sig." column of the PSPP output table.

Table 9: Chi-square tests Output for Race X Program Type

Statistic	Value	df	Asymp. Sig. (2-tailed)
Pearson Chi-Square	4.86	6	.56
Likelihood Ratio	4.91	6	.55
Linear-by-Linear Association	.50	1	.48
N of Valid Cases	200		

In the table representing SES by Program Type Crosstabs, we find that the calculated value of 16.60 (df 4) is greater than the critical value of 9.49 (see Chi square critical values in Appendix), so the differences are significant and should be explored further.

Table 10: Chi-square tests Output for SEs and Program Type

Statistic	Value	df	Asymp. Sig. (2-tailed)
Pearson Chi-Square	16.60	4	.00
Likelihood Ratio	16.78	4	.00
Linear-by-Linear Association	.06	1	.81
N of Valid Cases	200		

3. The "Asymp. Sig (2-tailed)" column will also give us the calculated p-value. A value of less than 0.05 can be considered significant. In this example the differences based on SES levels are significant (p<0.01).

Again it should be noted that the PSPP output tables will only show calculated p-values to two decimal places. Therefore any calculated values that appear as ".00", as displayed in our example output table above, should be reported as "p < 0.01".

4. Since we have found a statistically significant difference (p < 0.01) for Program Enrollment based on a student's socioeconomic status (SES), it is important to understand the impact, or magnitude of SES status on program enrollment.

Since this Chi Square Crosstabs Table has 3 rows and 3 columns we will use Cramer's Phi (ϕ_c) equation.

$$\phi_c = \sqrt{\frac{\chi2}{N(k-1)}}$$

In Cramer's Phi formula the $\chi2$ is equal to the Chi Square value produced by PSPP. The N is equal to the total number of total number of observances or samples. For k we use the lesser value from the number of rows or the number of columns.

The PSPP Chi Square output table contains all the values we need for this equation. From the table we find that $\chi2 = 16.6$, N = 200, and we will use k = 3 since this specific crosstabs table contains 3 rows and 3 columns.

$$\phi_c = \sqrt{\frac{16.6}{200(3-1)}} = \sqrt{\frac{16.6}{400}} = \sqrt{0.083} = 0.28$$

The effect size magnitude table (see appendix) suggests that this factor (student SES status) has a SMALL effect size. Therefore we can conclude that while the differences in program enrollment based on SES are statistically significant (p < 0.01), the effect size of a student's SES is small ($\phi_c = 0.28$).

Effect Size Calculation	Statistics Test	Small Effect	Medium Effect	Large Effect
Phi or Cramer's Phi	Chi Squared	0.1	0.3	0.5

Chi-Square Crosstabs Table Analysis

The Chi-square analysis does a very good job of indicating if there are statistically significant relationships or differences with categorical data. Those differences can be detected very easily if the categories only have two groups. But what if we have more than two groups within our categories? The chi-square can only tell us that there are some differences. We need to examine the Crosstabs Table to uncover where those differences may be present.

In our example we will conduct a chi-square analysis to determine if there are any relationships between a student's socioeconomic states (low, middle, or high) and enrollment in various program types (general, academic, or vocational tracks). The PSPP output window shows that there is a statistically significant difference in program type enrollment based on a student's socioeconomic status (SES), x^2 (4, N=200) = 16.60, p < 0.01.

Table 11: Chi-square tests

Statistic	Value	df	Asymp. Sig. (2-tailed)
Pearson Chi-Square	16.60	4	.00
N of Valid Cases	200		

But this is only part of the story. In the above example there are three categories for the Student SES level and three categories for their enrolled program type. How do we determine the significant differences?

One way to go about answering this question is by analyzing the Crosstabs Table that is also produced in the PSPP Output window.

Table 12: Socioeconomic Status * Program type [count, row %, column %, total %]

Socioeconomic Status	Program type general	academic	vocational	Total
low	16.00	19.00	12.00	47.00
	34.04%	40.43%	25.53%	100.00%
	35.56%	18.10%	24.00%	23.50%
	8.00%	9.50%	6.00%	23.50%
middle	20.00	44.00	31.00	95.00
	21.05%	46.32%	32.63%	100.00%
	44.44%	41.90%	62.00%	47.50%
	10.00%	22.00%	15.50%	47.50%
high	9.00	42.00	7.00	58.00
	15.52%	72.41%	12.07%	100.00%
	20.00%	40.00%	14.00%	29.00%
	4.50%	21.00%	3.50%	29.00%
Total	45.00	105.00	50.00	200.00
	22.50%	52.50%	25.00%	100.00%
	100.00%	100.00%	100.00%	100.00%
	22.50%	52.50%	25.00%	100.00%

Notice that in the Crosstabs table each row contains four lines. The first line indicates the count for that particular cell, the second line tells us the row percentage, the third line tells us the column percentage, and the fourth line is a total percentage.

Let us take a closer look at the first row of the table.

Table 13: Crosstabs Table Line 1

Socioeconomic Status * Program type [count, row %, column %, total %]

Socioeconomic Status	Program type general	academic	vocational	Total
low	16.00	19.00	12.00	47.00
	34.04%	40.43%	25.53%	100.00%
	35.56%	18.10%	24.00%	23.50%
	8.00%	9.50%	6.00%	23.50%

When we read Line 1 of the row we know that from the student population in the low SES group that 16 are enrolled in the general track program, 19 enrolled in the academic track program and 12 enrolled in the vocational track program. We also know that there were a total of 47 low SES students in this analysis.

Table 14: Crosstabs Table Line 2

Socioeconomic Status * Program type [count, row %, column %, total %]

Socioeconomic Status	Program type general	academic	vocational	Total
low	16.00	19.00	12.00	47.00
	34.04%	40.43%	25.53%	100.00%
	35.56%	18.10%	24.00%	23.50%
	8.00%	9.50%	6.00%	23.50%

In reviewing line 2, this tells us the percentages for the row. In other words, we can determine the percentage of low SES students within each program type. In this example we find that about 34% of the low SES students are enrolled in general programs, about 40.4% of low SES students are enrolled in academic programs, and about 25.5% of the low SES students are enrolled in the vocational program. The Total column tells us that we are accounting for 100% of the low SES students in the sample.

Table 15: Crosstabs Table Line 3

Socioeconomic Status * Program type [count, row %, column %, total %]

Socioeconomic Status	Program type general	academic	vocational	Total
low	16.00	19.00	12.00	47.00
	34.04%	40.43%	25.53%	100.00%
	35.56%	18.10%	24.00%	23.50%
	8.00%	9.50%	6.00%	23.50%

In reviewing line 3 of the Crosstabs table, we can determine the percentage of low SES students enrolled in each program type compared to the other SES groups. In our example about 35.5% of the general program track is comprised of the low SES students, about 18% of the academic program track is comprised of low SES students, and about 24% of the vocational program track is comprised of low SES students. The last column tells us that the low SES student group accounts for about 23% of the total population sample.

Table 16: Crosstabs Table Line 4

Socioeconomic Status * Program type [count, row %, column %, total %]

Socioeconomic Status	Program type general	academic	vocational	Total
low	16.00	19.00	12.00	47.00
	34.04%	40.43%	25.53%	100.00%
	35.56%	18.10%	24.00%	23.50%
	8.00%	9.50%	6.00%	23.50%

Line 4 of each row indicates the percentage as compared to the entire sample population. In this example we find that the low SES students enrolled in general programs are about 8% of the entire sample, the low SES students enrolled in academic programs are about 9.5% of the entire sample, and the low SES students enrolled in vocational programs are about 6% of the entire sample.

The columns of the Crosstabs table can be interpreted in a similar way.

Table 17: Crosstabs Table Columns

Socioeconomic Status * Program type [count, row %, column %, total %]

Socioeconomic Status	Program type general	academic	vocational	Total
low	16.00	19.00	12.00	47.00
	34.04%	40.43%	25.53%	100.00%
	35.56%	18.10%	24.00%	23.50%
	8.00%	9.50%	6.00%	23.50%
middle	20.00	44.00	31.00	95.00
	21.05%	46.32%	32.63%	100.00%
	44.44%	41.90%	62.00%	47.50%
	10.00%	22.00%	15.50%	47.50%

high	9.00	42.00	7.00	58.00
	15.52%	72.41%	12.07%	100.00%
	20.00%	40.00%	14.00%	29.00%
	4.50%	21.00%	3.50%	29.00%
Total	45.00	105.00	50.00	200.00
	22.50%	52.50%	25.00%	100.00%
	100.00%	100.00%	100.00%	100.00%
	22.50%	52.50%	25.00%	100.00%

If we examine the general program column, line 3 gives us information about the students from our three SES categories and their enrollment percentage in that program category. Here we find that about 35.5% of the general program enrollment is comprised of students from the low SES category, about 44.4% of the general program enrollment is comprised of students from the middle SES category, and about 22.5% of the general program enrollment is comprised of students from the high SES category. In the last row of the table, line 3 indicates that we have accounted for 100% of the general category enrollment.

We can analysis each column of the Crosstabs table in a similar process.

Another strategy to interpreting the Crosstabs table is to identify percentages that seem to have the most prominent differences. We can then "read" that cell to make some meaning from the results.

In the example below we focus on some percentages that stand out from the rest.

Table 18: Crosstabs Table Percentages

Socioeconomic Status * Program type [count, row %, column %, total %]

Socioeconomic Status	Program type general	academic	vocational	Total
low	16.00	19.00	12.00	47.00
	34.04%	40.43%	25.53%	100.00%
	35.56%	18.10%		23.50%
	8.00%	9.50%	6.00%	23.50%
middle	20.00	44.00	31.00	95.00
	21.05%	46.32%	32.63%	100.00%
	44.44%	41.90%	62.00%	47.50%
	10.00%	22.00%	15.50%	47.50%
high	9.00	42.00	7.00	58.00
		72.41%	12.07%	100.00%
	20.00%	40.00%	14.00%	29.00%
	4.50%	21.00%	3.50%	29.00%
Total	45.00	105.00	50.00	200.00
	22.50%	52.50%	25.00%	100.00%
	100.00%	100.00%	100.00%	100.00%
	22.50%	52.50%	25.00%	100.00%

An examination of the Crosstabs table reveals that the academic program is comprised of about 18% of low SES students, as read in line 3 of low SES row. Also we find that the vocational program is comprised of about 14% of high SES students, as seen in line 3 of the high SES row. Finally the table reveals that about 74% of the high SES students are enrolled in the academic track program. These findings may warrant further research and analysis.

Chapter 8
Relationship Analysis with t-Test

t-Test Analysis (Continuous Differences, two groups)

The Student's t-Test is used to determine if differences between values of continuous data are significant when comparing two factors, or groups within the data. Factors are the descriptive feature of the data, such as gender, SES, race, etc. With the t-Test, regardless of how many factors or groups are in your data, the t-Test will only compare two of those factors at one time.

There are three t-Tests methods available in PSPP;

1. **One Sample t-Test**: Compares the mean score of a sample to a known mean score. The known mean is typically referred to as the population mean.
2. **Independent Samples t-Test**: Compares the means scores of two groups on a given variable.
3. **Pair Samples t-Test**: Compares the means of two variables. This is commonly used for groups with pre- and post- variables.

Using the t-Test Distribution Table

The distribution table enables the PSPP t-value to be compared to the critical value to determine if the differences are significant.

- Use the column with the probability or confidence level that you want. The confidence level of 0.05 is most commonly used in social science research.
- Select the proper row for the degrees of freedom (df) in your data. The df will be shown in the PSPP output table.
- Compare the value from your output table with the critical value table.
- The results are significant if the calculated t-value is *greater* than the critical value.

Degrees of Freedom	Probability, p			
	0.1	0.05	0.01	0.001
1	6.31	12.71	63.66	636.62
2	2.92	4.30	9.93	31.60
3	2.35	3.18	5.84	12.92
4	2.13	2.78	4.60	8.61
5	2.02	2.57	4.03	6.87
6	1.94	2.45	3.71	5.96
7	1.89	2.37	3.50	5.41
8	1.86	2.31	3.36	5.04
9	1.83	2.26	3.25	4.78
10	1.81	2.23	3.17	4.59
12	1.78	2.18	3.06	4.32
14	1.76	2.14	2.98	4.14
16	1.75	2.12	2.92	4.02
17	1.74	2.11	2.90	3.97
18	1.73	2.10	2.88	3.92
19	1.73	2.09	2.86	3.88
20	1.72	2.09	2.85	3.85

Figure 66: Sample t-Table of Critical Values

Independent Samples t-Test using PSPP

1. Using the menu, select Analyze>Compare Means>T-Test. Be sure to select the correct t-Test for your data set. In this case we are using the Independent Samples t-Test. With Independent Samples we will investigate the differences between TWO groups on the SAME measure.

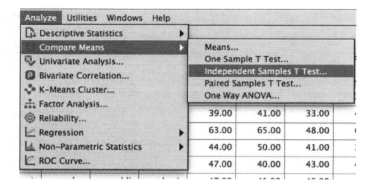

Figure 67: PSPP Independent Samples t-Test Menu

2. When using the Independent Samples t-Test select the test variable and the groups. Be sure to define the two groups from within the variable. Click "Define Groups" and enter the codes used for the two groups to be compared. Check your codebook to be sure you are using the correct values for your comparison groups.

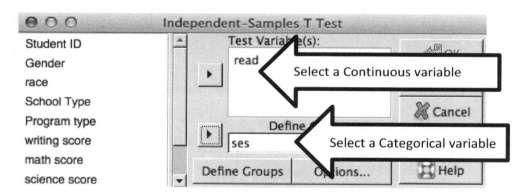

Figure 68: Independent t-Test Sample Window

3. Define the two groups in your categorical data set that will be compared. In this example we have selected SES and will compare groups 1 and 4, which in the codebook corresponds to "Hispanic" students and "White" students respectively.

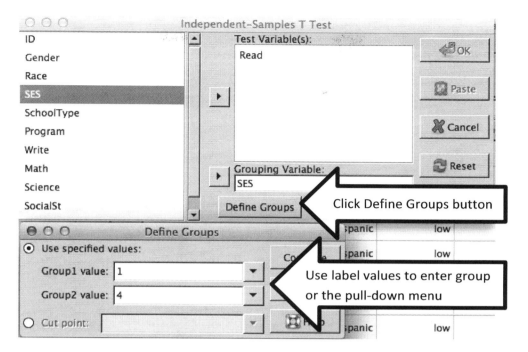

Figure 69: Defining Groups for t-Test

4. Determine if the variance of the two groups is significant. If conducting an Independent Sample t-Test, we use the Levene's Test of Equality of Variances to determine if the difference in variation is significant. The Levene's Test value directs us to which line in the output table to use in our analysis.

5. If the Levene's Test is not significant ("Sig." value is greater than .05), then equal variances can be assumed and the two variances are not significantly different and we read the values in the **first line** of the table. If the Lenene's Test is significant (the value under "Sig." value is less than .05), then equal variances are not assumed and the two variances are significantly different and we read the values from the **second line** in the table.

Levene's Test is simply a measure of how much variation is present in our data set. Data with a lot of variation undergoes one statistical process while data with very little variation can be put to other statistical tests. PSPP handles this for us and produces both results.

This is one of the few times that a researcher hopes for values that are not significant because this will indicate that the data set has equal variances.

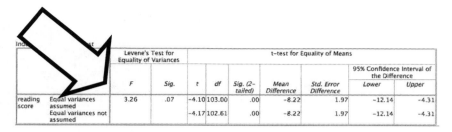

		Levene's Test for Equality of Variances		t-test for Equality of Means						
									95% Confidence Interval of the Difference	
		F	Sig.	t	df	Sig. (2-tailed)	Mean Difference	Std. Error Difference	Lower	Upper
reading score	Equal variances assumed	3.26	.07	-4.10	103.00	.00	-8.22	1.97	-12.14	-4.31
	Equal variances not assumed			-4.17	102.61	.00	-8.22	1.97	-12.14	-4.31

Figure 70: t-Test Output Window for Levene's Test

6. View the output window. Locate the t-value and degrees of freedom (df) from the output table. Compare this value to the t-Test distribution table.

In reviewing the Independent Samples output table be sure to use the row that is indicated by the Levene's test. The first row, "Equal variances assumed" is used when the value for the Levene's test is NOT significant. The second row, "Equal variances not assumed", is used when the values for Levene's test IS significant.

```
T-TEST /VARIABLES= Read
    /GROUPS=Gender(0,1)   /MISSING=ANALYSIS
    /CRITERIA=CIN(0.95).
```

Group Statistics

	Gender	N	Mean	Std. Deviation	S.E. Mean
Read	male	91	52.82	10.51	1.10
	female	109	51.73	10.06	.96

Independent Samples Test

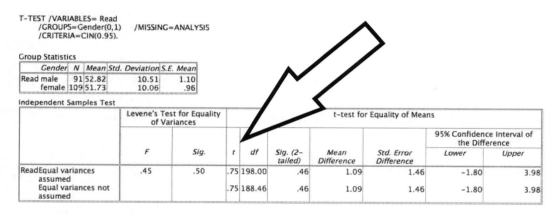

		Levene's Test for Equality of Variances		t-test for Equality of Means						
									95% Confidence Interval of the Difference	
		F	Sig.	t	df	Sig. (2-tailed)	Mean Difference	Std. Error Difference	Lower	Upper
Read	Equal variances assumed	.45	.50	.75	198.00	.46	1.09	1.46	-1.80	3.98
	Equal variances not assumed			.75	188.46	.46	1.09	1.46	-1.80	3.98

Figure 71: t-Test output table for differences on reading scores by gender

7. If the calculated t-value is greater than the critical value (see t-test critical values in Appendix) from the distribution table, then the differences are statistically significant. If the value is less than the critical value from the table then the differences are not significant.

8. The t-Test output tables, as shown in the Independent Samples Test table above, also displays the calculated p-value for the test in the column labeled "Sig. (2-tailed)". We can determine if the differences are statistically significantly from this column of the output table.

Interpreting Output Tables: Independent Samples t-Test

In this example we have an Independent Samples t-Test output table to determine if there are differences in Science Test scores between the low SES level students and the high SES level students.

```
T-TEST /VARIABLES= Science
    /GROUPS=SES(1,3)  /MISSING=ANALYSIS
    /CRITERIA=CIN(0.95).
```

Group Statistics

	SES	N	Mean	Std. Deviation	S.E. Mean
Science	low	47	47.70	10.41	1.52
	high	58	55.45	9.79	1.29

Independent Samples Test

		Levene's Test for Equality of Variances		t-test for Equality of Means						
									95% Confidence Interval of the Difference	
		F	Sig.	t	df	Sig. (2-tailed)	Mean Difference	Std. Error Difference	Lower	Upper
Science	Equal variances assumed	.86	.36	-3.92	103.00	.00	-7.75	1.99	-11.69	-3.80
	Equal variances not assumed			-3.89	95.85	.00	-7.75	1.99	-11.70	-3.80

Figure 72: t-Test output table for science scores & SES

1. We begin by looking at the "Levene's Test for Equality of Variances". If the significance value (Sig. column of the table) is greater than 0.05, meaning that the differences in variance are not significant, then we use the first row of the output table. If the value is less than 0.05, meaning that the differences in variance are significant, then we use the second row of the output table.

Table 19: t-Test Output Table for SES and Science Scores (Levene's test)

		Levene's Test for Equality of Variances				
		F	Sig.	t	df	Sig. (2-tailed)
science score	Equal variances assumed	.86	.36	-3.92	103.00	.00
	Equal variances not assumed			-3.89	95.85	.00

In this example the value is 0.36 which is greater than our selected confidence level of 0.05, therefore we can use the first row labeled "Equal variances assumed". If this value had been below 0.05 we would review the t-value from the second line "Equal variances not assumed".

2. In determining if the differences between the groups is significant we us the t-value and the degrees of freedom (df) from the appropriate row of the output table. These values can be compared to the critical values found on t-Test table of critical values. If the calculated value from the output table is greater than the critical value then the difference is significant. For comparison with the table values we use the "absolute value" of the calculated t-value. In this case we would find that the t-value of $|-3.92|$, or 3.92, with 103 df is greater than the critical value of 1.98 (see t-test critical values in Appendix) from the table, so the differences are statistically significant.

3. The "Asymp. Sig (2-tailed)" column will also give us the calculated p-value. A value of less than 0.05 can also be considered significant. In this example the calculated p-value of ".00" indicates that $p < 0.01$.

As noted earlier, the PSPP output tables will only show calculated p-values to two decimal places. Therefore any calculated values that appear as ".00", as displayed in our example output table above, should be reported as "$p < 0.01$".

Table 20: t-Test Output Table for SES and Science Scores (t-value)

| | | Levene's Test for Equality of Variances | | | | |
		F	Sig.	t	df	Sig. (2-tailed)
science score	Equal variances assumed	.86	.36	-3.92	103.00	.00
	Equal variances not assumed			-3.89	95.85	.00

4. The Confidence Interval also gives us an important measure of statistical significance. When using the t-Test to compare the means of two groups, the hypothetical difference between the means would be zero (0).

The output table for Independent Samples t-Test will show the mean interval difference at the 95% confidence level. The range of means displayed shows the upper and lower values of what we believe the differences to be within this sample. In this example (see the table below) we note that the mean difference range is from 3.80 to 11.69 for our two selected student groups.

If the confidence level DOES NOT contain zero (0) we may reject the null hypothesis that the mean difference is zero and note that the differences are statistically significant. If the confidence interval had CONTAINED zero (0), then we would probably have failed to reject the null hypothesis and concluded that there were not statistically significant differences between the means.

Table 21: Output for Independent Samples with Confidence Interval

| | | Levene's Test for Equality of Variances | | t-test for Equality of Means | | | | | 95% Confidence Interval of the Difference | |
		F	Sig.	t	df	Sig. (2-tailed)	Mean Difference	Std. Error Difference	Lower	Upper
science score	Equal variances assumed	.86	.36	3.92	103.00	.00	7.75	1.99	3.80	11.69
	Equal variances not assumed			3.89	95.85	.00	7.75	1.99	3.80	11.70

5. Now that we have determined that the difference in science assessment scores between high SES students and low SES students is statistically significant (p < 0.01), we will want to find the magnitude of SES on science scores.

In this example we used an Independent Samples t-Test, therefore we will use the equation for Cohen's d with pooled standard deviation calculated.

$$d = \frac{mean_2 - mean_1}{SD_{pooled}}, \text{SD pooled} = \sqrt{\frac{(SD_{group1})^2 + (SD_{group2})^2}{2}}$$

In order to calculate Cohen's d we must find the mean and standard deviation (SD) for each group used in the analysis. The science scores for the low SES students were $mean_1$ = 47.70 and the SD_{group1} = 10.41. The science scores for the high SES students were $mean_2$ = 55.45 and the SD_{group2} = 9.79.

Calculate the pooled standard deviation.

$$\text{SD pooled} = \sqrt{\frac{(SD_{group1})^2 + (SD_{group2})^2}{2}} = \sqrt{\frac{10.41^2 + 9.79^2}{2}} = \sqrt{102.1} = 10.11$$

We can now use the SD_{pooled} value in the equation for Cohen's d.

$$d = \frac{55.45-47.70}{10.11} = 0.76$$

From the effect size magnitude table (see appendix) this would be considered a LARGE effect size. So a student's SES status had a large effect on Science scores.

Effect Size Calculation	Statistics Test	Small Effect	Medium Effect	Large Effect
Cohen's d	t-Test (Paired & Independent)	0.2	0.5	0.8

The effect size chart shows us that the midpoint of the large effect size for Cohen's d is 0.8. If we think of these values as the midpoint of a range, then the large effect size would be from approximately 0.65 and greater. Therefore our calculated effect size in this example of 0.76 would fall just below the midpoint of the large effect size range and above the lower value for the large effect size range.

We could also determine the effect size for an Independent Samples t-Test with the r^2 calculation. From the PSPP Output Table we find that t = -3.92 and df = 103.

$$r^2 = \frac{t^2}{(t^2+df)} = \frac{(-3.92)^2}{((-3.92)^2+103)} = 0.13$$

Effect Size Calculation	Statistics Test	Small Effect	Medium Effect	Large Effect
r^2	t-Test (Independent)	0.01	0.09	0.25

From the effect size magnitude table (see appendix) this would also be considered a Medium effect size at the upper end of the range.

Paired Samples t-Test using PSPP

1. Using the menu, select Analyze>Compare Means>T-Test. Be sure to select the correct t-Test for your data set. In this case we are using the Paired Samples t-Test. With Paired (Dependent) Samples we will investigate the differences between ONE group on the TWO different measures, such as two assessments or a pre-/post-assessment.

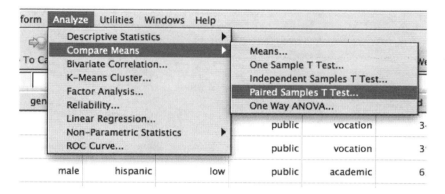

Figure 73: PSPP t-Test Menu

2. When using the Paired Samples t-Test, in the dialogue box you will need to select the TWO variables. Use the arrow to move each variable into "Test Pair(s) window".

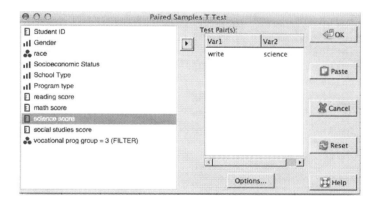

Figure 74: Paired Samples t-Test Window

3. View the output window. Locate the t-value and degrees of freedom (df) from the output table. Compare this value to the t-Test distribution table.

```
T-TEST
    PAIRS = write WITH science (PAIRED)
    /MISSING=ANALYSIS
    /CRITERIA=CIN(0.95).
```

Paired Sample Statistics

	Mean	N	Std. Deviation	S.E. Mean
Pair 1 writing score	52.77	200	9.48	.67
science score	51.36	200	9.91	.70

Paired Samples Correlations

	N	Correlation	Sig.
Pair 1 writing score & science score	200	.52	.00

Paired Samples Test

	Paired Differences					t	df	Sig. (2–tailed)
	Mean	Std. Deviation	Std. Error Mean	95% Confidence Interval of the Difference				
				Lower	Upper			
Pair 1 writing score – science score	1.42	9.53	.67	.09	2.74	2.10	199	.04

Figure 75: t-Test output table for differences on writing and science.

4. If the calculated t-value is greater than the critical value (see t-test critical values in Appendix) from the distribution table, then the differences are statistically significant. If the value is less than the critical value from the table then the differences are not significant.

5. The t-Test output tables, as shown in the Paired Samples Test table above, also displays the calculated significance level for the test in the column labeled "Sig. (2-tailed)". In this example the p-value equals 0.04.

We could conclude from this example that the students scored significantly different on the writing test than they scored on the science test.

Interpreting Output Tables: Paired Samples t-Test

In this example we have an Paired Samples t-Test output table to determine if there are differences in Science Test scores and Writing Test scores.

```
T-TEST
     PAIRS = write WITH science (PAIRED)
     /MISSING=ANALYSIS
     /CRITERIA=CIN(0.95).
```

Paired Sample Statistics

	Mean	N	Std. Deviation	S.E. Mean
Pair 1 writing score	52.77	200	9.48	.67
science score	51.36	200	9.91	.70

Paired Samples Correlations

	N	Correlation	Sig.
Pair 1 writing score & science score	200	.52	.00

Paired Samples Test

	Paired Differences					t	df	Sig. (2-tailed)
	Mean	Std. Deviation	Std. Error Mean	95% Confidence Interval of the Difference				
				Lower	Upper			
Pair 1 writing score – science score	1.42	9.53	.67	.09	2.74	2.10	199	.04

Figure 76: t-Test output table for science scores & SES

1. In determining if the differences between the tests is significant we use the calculated t-value and the degrees of freedom (df) from the appropriate row of the output table. These values can be compared to the critical values found on t-Test table of critical values. If the calculated value from the output table is greater than the critical value then the difference is significant. For comparison with the table values we use the "absolute value" of the calculated t-value. In this case we would find that the t-value of 2.10, with 199 df is greater than the critical value of 1.97 (see t-test critical values in Appendix) from the table, so the differences are statistically significant.

Table 22: t-Test Output Table for Writing and Science Scores (t-value)

	Paired Differences							
				95% Confidence Interval of the Difference				
	Mean	*Std. Deviation*	*Std. Error Mean*	*Lower*	*Upper*	*t*	*df*	*Sig. (2-tailed)*
Pair 1 writing score - science score	1.42	9.53	.67	.09	2.74	2.10	199	.04

2. The output table for the Paired Samples t-Test also indicates that these results are statistically significant as shown in the "Sig. (2-tailed)" column. The p -value is shown to be p < 0.05. In reviewing the output table we find that the actual calculated p-value is "0.04" which is very close to our critical value.

3. The Confidence Interval also gives us an important measure of statistical significance. When using the t-Test to compare the means of two measures, the hypothetical difference between the means would be zero (0).

The output table for Paired Samples t-Test will show the mean interval difference at the 95% confidence level. This is the mean range displaying is the upper and lower values of what we believe the differences to be within this sample. In this example we note that the mean difference range is from 0.09 to 2.74 for the writing and science scores.

If the confidence level DOES NOT contain zero (0) we may reject the null hypothesis that the mean difference is zero and note that the differences could be statistically significant. If the confidence interval had CONTAINED zero (0), then we would probably fail to reject the null hypothesis and concluded that there were not statistically significant differences between the means.

Table 23: t-Test Output Table with Confidence Interval (t-value)

	Paired Differences							
				95% Confidence Interval of the Difference				
	Mean	*Std. Deviation*	*Std. Error Mean*	*Lower*	*Upper*	*t*	*df*	*Sig. (2-tailed)*
Pair 1 writing score - science score	1.42	9.53	.67	.09	2.74	2.10	199	.04

However it should be noted that if we review both the p-value and the confidence interval, these two values may be problematic. The calculated p-value for this sample was very close to our critical value of 0.05, in fact the calculated p-value was only 0.04. Also with the confidence interval, even though the interval does not contain zero within the values it is very close to zero with the lower end of the values at 0.09.

4. Given the calculated p-value and the confidence interval above we will now determine the effect size for the Paired Samples t-Test using the Cohen's d equation.

$$d = \frac{mean_2 - mean_1}{standard\ deviation\ (SD)} = \frac{mean\ difference}{standard\ deviation\ (SD)}$$

In this example all of the necessary values can be found in the Paired Samples t-Test output table. From the table we find that the "mean" is 1.41. The table column is labeled as "mean" however the value shown is the mean difference. The standard deviation is 9.53.

$$d = \frac{1.41}{9.53} = 0.15$$

Be careful in reading the PSPP output tables. We DO NOT want to use the mean and standard deviation values from the "Paired Samples Statistics" table, but rather from the "Paired Samples Test" table (see Figure 76).

The effect size magnitude table (see appendix) suggests that this is a SMALL effect size. In this case we found that the p-value equal to 0.04 which is less that our critical value of 0.05, but not by much. We also find that the effect is small suggesting that the differences found between these two assessment samples may not have much practical meaning.

Effect Size Calculation	Statistics Test	Small Effect	Medium Effect	Large Effect
Cohen's d	t-Test (Paired)	0.2	0.5	0.8

Chapter 9
Relationship Analysis with ANOVA

Analysis of Variance (ANOVA)

The Analysis of Variance (ANOVA) is used to find differences between continuous variables with multiple groups (the independent factor) and a dependent variable such as a test score. This can be thought of as performing multiple t-Tests at one time. When using the t-Test we must specify the two groups within a variable that will be compared, however in using an ANOVA test we can consider all the groups at once.

One-Way ANOVA

A One-Way ANOVA will compare the means of multiple groups with a single dependent variable. This analysis will uncover differences between the groups. If we have a hypothesis as to which groups are interacting we can also perform a contrasts analysis within the ANOVA test. The use of Contrast Analysis will be discussed in depth later in the chapter.

1. In PSPP use the Analyze menu to select the One-Way ANOVA. This is accomplished by selecting Analyze > Compare Means > One Way ANOVA.

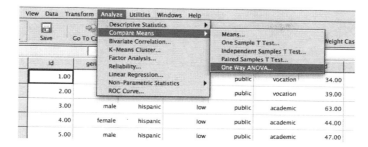

Figure 77: One Way ANOVA Menu

2. From the dialog box we will select the dependent and independent variables. The dependent variable, in the case of our sample data set, will be continuous data (one of the test scores). In this example we have chosen to examine the reading scores.

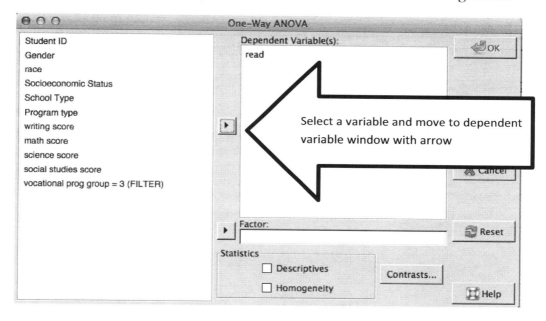

Figure 78: One Way ANOVA Dialogue Window

3. Then from the same dialogue box select the independent variable. This will be one of the categorical data sets that contain more than two groups. In this example we have selected "SES".

Note: It would not be useful to choose an independent data set that only had two groups, such as "gender" since a simple t-Test can handle comparisons between two groups.

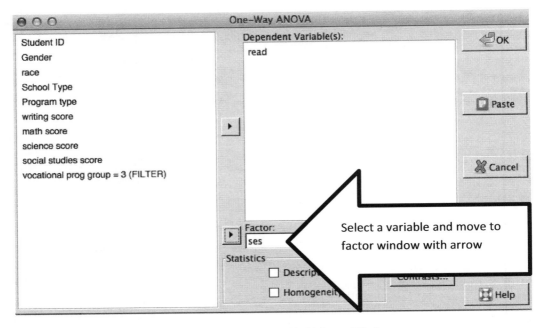

Figure 79: One Way ANOVA Dialogue Window

In the dialog window, check both the "Descriptives" and "Homogeneity" settings in the Statistics section.

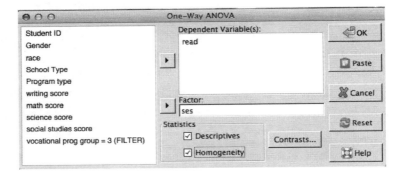

Figure 80: One Way ANOVA

4. Click "OK" in the dialogue window. The ANOVA tables will be produced in the Output Window.

5. The results of the One-Way ANOVA can be viewed in the Output window.

Interpreting Output Tables: One-Way ANOVA

Once you run the One-Way ANOVA, the results will be in the Output Window of PSPP.

Descriptives

		N	Mean	Std. Deviation	Std. Error	95% Confidence Interval for Mean		Minimum	Maximum
						Lower Bound	Upper Bound		
reading score	low	47	48.28	9.34	1.36	45.53	51.02	28.00	68.00
	middle	95	51.58	9.43	.97	49.66	53.50	31.00	73.00
	high	58	56.50	10.86	1.43	53.64	59.36	34.00	76.00
	Total	200	52.23	10.25	.72	50.80	53.66	28.00	76.00

Test of Homogeneity of Variances

	Levene Statistic	df1	df2	Sig.
reading score	2.44	2	197	.09

ANOVA

		Sum of Squares	df	Mean Square	F	Sig.
reading score	Between Groups	1832.36	2	916.18	9.46	.00
	Within Groups	19087.06	197	96.89		
	Total	20919.42	199			

Figure 81: One Way ANOVA Output Table for Reading Scores and SES

From the output table we have a few sections to use in our analysis.

1. The table containing the "Test of Homogeneity of Variances" gives us the Levene Statistic measuring variation within the data. If the Levene's Test is not significant ("Sig." value is greater than .05), then **equal variances can be assumed** and the two variances are not significantly different. If it is significant (the value under "Sig." value is less than .05), then **equal variances are not assumed** and the two variances are significantly different. We will learn more about using the Levene Statistic when Contrasts are discussed later in the chapter.

2. The ANOVA output table will display the F-value. We also need both degrees of freedom values that will be shown in the df column of the table. We use the df values from the "Between Groups" row and the "Within Groups" row. The ANOVA table will produce an F-value for this statistic. With the F-value and the degrees of freedom (df) we can look up the critical value in an F-Table of Values. If the test value is greater than the critical value there is a difference within the data and it is significant. In this example the calculated value of 9.46 is greater than the critical value of 3.04 from the F-Table (see appendix for F Table of Critical Values) so we can state that the differences are significant, however, without the contrast table we would not know which groups were interacting to make the differences.

Table 24: ANOVA Output Table

		Sum of Squares	df	Mean Square	F	Sig.
reading score	Between Groups	1832.36	2	916.18	9.46	.00
	Within Groups	19087.06	197	96.89		
	Total	20919.42	199			

It should be noted that the PSPP output tables will only show calculated p-values to two decimal places. Therefore any calculated values that appear as ".00" and the significance should be reported as "p < 0.01".

3. The ANOVA table indicates that there are statistically significant differences in reading scores based on a student's SES level. The question that remains is which groups or groupings account for these differences. The statistics here merely tells us that there are differences. We will need further analysis to determine which group interactions account for the differences.

4. We can review the Confidence Intervals in the One-Way ANOVA output table to determine the differences between our groups. These "confidence intervals" provide us with an interval estimate on the range of values that we could expect our true mean value to fall. When the confidence intervals of our groups DO NOT overlap, we can be at least 95% confident that there is statistically significant differences in the means of these groups.

Table 25: Confidence Interval Ranges

		N	Mean	Std. Deviation	Std. Error	95% Confidence Interval for Mean Lower Bound	95% Confidence Interval for Mean Upper Bound	Minimum	Maximum
reading score	low	47	48.28	9.34	1.36	45.53	51.02	28.00	68.00
	middle	95	51.58	9.43	.97	49.66	53.50	31.00	73.00
	high	58	56.50	10.86	1.43	53.64	59.36	34.00	76.00
	Total	200	52.23	10.25	.72	50.80	53.66	28.00	76.00

5. In this example at the 95% confidence level, we would expect the mean reading score for the low SES group to be between 45.53 and 51.02, the middle SES group to be between 49.66 and 53.50, and the high SES group to be between 53.64 and 59.36.

The expected range of means for the high SES group DOES NOT overlap with either the low or middle SES groups. Therefore we could expect there to be a statistically significant difference between the high SES group and the other two groups. We can also notice that the expected ranges for the middle and low SES groups DO overlap, so we would not expect there to be a statistically significant difference between the means of these two groups.

6. In this example we have found that the difference in Reading scores based on a student's SES is probably statistically significant, as suggested by the "Interval for Means". Now we will examine the magnitude of those differences by calculating the effect size.

The effect size for a One-Way ANOVA is calculated by using the eta squared equation.

$$\eta^2 = \frac{SS_{between\ groups}}{SS_{total}}$$

The Sum of Squares for "Between Groups" and "Total" is taken directly from the PSPP ANOVA output table. In this example we find that the Sum of Squares Between Groups is 1832.36 and the Sum of Squares Total is 20,919.42.

$$\eta^2 = \frac{1832.36}{20919.42} = 0.09$$

The effect size magnitude table (see appendix) suggests that this is a LARGE effect. So we can conclude that the difference in reading scores between the student High SES groups when compared to the Low and Middle student SES groups does have a statistical significance ($p < 0.01$) with a large effect size ($d = 0.09$).

Effect Size Calculation	Statistics Test	Small Effect	Medium Effect	Large Effect
Eta Squared	ANOVA	0.01	0.06	0.14

7. We find in this example that there is a statistically significant difference in Reading test scores, $F_{(2, 197)} = 9.46$, $p < 0.01$, between the students in the high SES group when compared to the other two student groups ($\eta^2 = 0.09$).

Introduction to Planned Contrasts

As we have seen in the introduction to ANOVA analysis, the output tables are helpful in determining if any significant differences exists among our groups, however it does not directly inform us as to which groups represent the most significant differences.

The "Confidence Interval for the Mean" output table produced by PSPP can help suggest which groups may have the statistically significant differences

The use of either Planned Contrasts analysis or Post Hoc analysis can help the researcher determines which groups are interacting. When we have a hypothesis about these interactions in mind, then conducting a Planned Contrasts test can determine if the hypothesis is accurate or not. Often the "Confidence Interval for the Mean" table will suggest possible hypothesis to test.

When we do not have a specific hypothesis to test, perhaps the Confidence Intervals are just too close together to suggest a specific interaction, then Post Hoc analysis will test every possible hypothesis with specific pairings of groups that contain the most significant differences. The current version of PSPP does not contain Post Hoc analysis as a native function. There are Post Hoc calculators online.

Conducting One-Way ANOVA with Planned Contrasts

Analysis of Variance (ANOVA) is a powerful technique to find relationships and differences when our data has more than two categories. The ANOVA results itself will indicate if the differences are statistically significant. Conducting an ANOVA with Planned Contrasts may reveal which groups or groupings are different.

ANOVA with Planned Contrasts is a way to conduct hypothesis testing with the various groupings within your data. PSPP can support up to 10 contrasts analysis. For example, if we consider our sample data we may want to know of there are any relationships or differences in the student math scores based on student socioeconomic status (SES).

The ANOVA will reveal that there are differences in math scores based on a student's SES level, $F (2, 197) = 7.97$, $p < 0.01$. However these results do not tell us which groups or groupings have these differences. The Confidence Interval for the Mean may help suggest some differences.

		N	Mean	95% Confidence Interval for Mean	
				Lower Bound	*Upper Bound*
math score	low	47	49.17	46.56	51.78
	middle	95	52.21	50.30	54.12
	high	58	56.17	53.89	58.46
	Total	200	52.64	51.34	53.95

In this example at the 95% confidence level, we would expect the mean math score for the low SES group to be between 45.56 and 51.78, the middle SES group to be between 50.30 and 54.12, and the high SES group to be between 53.89 and 58.46.

Because the mean intervals for the low and middle SES groups overlap one another we would not expect there to be a significant difference in the scores. However the high SES group mean interval does not overlap with either the low or middle SES groups. Therefore our hypothesis could be that there exists a significant difference in math scores between the high SES group and the other two student groups.

This is where the planned contrasts can help us answer the question of significant differences among groups. In the table below is an example of the groupings we may wish to test.

Table 26: Planned Contrasts for SES Level differences on Math scores

	Contrast 1	Contrast 2	Contrast 3	Contrast 4	Contrast 5
Grouping	Low	Low-Middle	Low	Low	Middle
Compared to	Middle-High	High	Middle	High	High

In order to create the groupings within PSPP, each Contrast will be assigned an integer variable or coefficient. Categories with the same coefficient will be considered one group. Categories with inverse coefficients will be considered as part of the comparison group. Any category that is assigned a coefficient of zero (0) will not be considered in the analysis. And finally, when we add all the coefficients together the sum must be zero (0).

The following table illustrates the coefficient assignments that we could make for the Planned Contrasts testing for differences in math scores based on student SES levels.

Table 27: Contrast Variable Assignments for SES Level differences on Math scores

	Variable Assignments				
	Contrast 1	Contrast 2	Contrast 3	Contrast 4	Contrast 5
Low	2	1	1	1	0
Middle	-1	1	0	-1	1
High	-1	-2	-1	0	-1
What does this contrast mean?	Low SES compared to Middle & High as a group	Low & Middle SES as a group compared to High SES	Low SES compared to High SES. Middle SES not considered	Low SES compared to Middle SES. High SES not considered	Middle SES compared to High SES. Low SES not considered

Notice how the coefficients are arranged for these contrasts. In Contrast 1 we want to treat the Low SES category as one group and the Middle-High SES categories as another grouping. In the contrast table we assign the Low SES category a coefficient equal to "2" while both the Middle and High SES categories are assigned coefficients equal to "-1". The sum of all the contrast coefficients is equal to zero (0).

Another example of using the contrast coefficients to exclude one category from the analysis is shown in Contrast 3. Here we want to only compare the Low SES group to the High SES group without considering the Middle SES group in the analysis. In Contrast 3 we want to treat the Low SES category as one group and the High SES categories as another group. In the contrast table we assign the Low SES category a coefficient equal to "1" while the High SES category is assigned a coefficient equal to "-1". The Middle SES category is assigned a coefficient of "0" or zero. Again, the sum of all the contrast coefficients is equal to zero (0).

Steps to Conduct ANOVA with Planned Contrasts in PSPP

1. From the PSPP menu, select Analyze > Compare Means > One Way ANOVA.

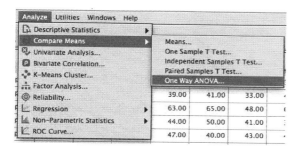

2. Move the test variable into the "Dependent Variable" window, in this example we will move "math" scores into the dependent variable window, and the categories to consider into the "Factor" window, which will be the SES level in this example. Be sure that both "Descriptives" and "Homogeneity" are checked in the Statistics window.

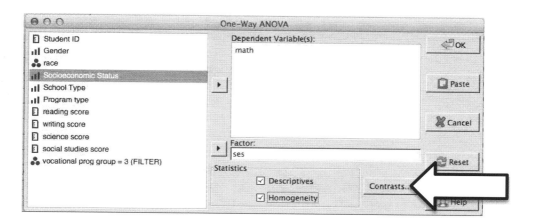

3. Next, click on the "Contrasts" button.

4. In the dialog window you will enter all the coefficients for your planned contrasts. The variables are entered in the same order that they were created in PSPP. In the case of our example, PSPP has the SES categories in order as Low, Middle, and High. Enter the first coefficient, then click the "Add" button. Enter the second coefficient, then click the "Add" button. Continue until all the coefficients have been entered for the first contrast test.

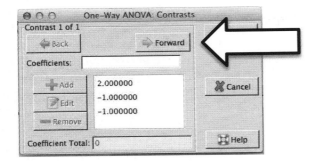

5. To enter the next planned contrasts, click the "Forward" button. This will bring up "Contrast 2 of 2". Enter all the coefficients for this contrast test.

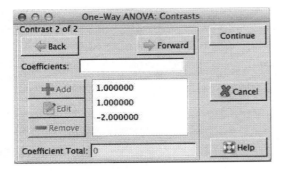

6. Continue entering all the planned contrast coefficients. After they have all been entered click on the "Continue" button.

7. Click "OK" to conduct the ANOVA with Planned Contrasts analysis.

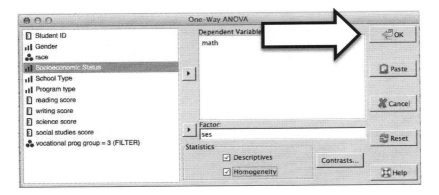

Analyzing the ANOVA Output Tables with Contrasts

Once the ANOVA with Planned Contrasts has been conducted, go to the PSPP Output Window to interpret the results.

Test of Homogeneity of Variances

	Levene Statistic	df1	df2	Sig.
math score	.14	2	197	.87

ANOVA

		Sum of Squares	df	Mean Square	F	Sig.
math score	Between Groups	1307.09	2	653.55	7.97	.00
	Within Groups	16158.70	197	82.02		
	Total	17465.80	199			

Contrast Coefficients

		Socioeconomic Status		
		low	middle	high
Contrast	1	2	−1	−1
	2	1	1	−2
	3	1	0	−1
	4	1	−1	0
	5	0	1	−1

Contrast Tests

		Contrast	Value of Contrast	Std. Error	t	df	Sig. (2-tailed)
math score	Assume equal variances	1	−10.04	3.04	3.30	197	.00
		2	−10.96	2.87	3.81	197	.00
		3	−7.00	1.78	3.94	197	.00
		4	−3.04	1.62	1.88	197	.06
		5	−3.96	1.51	2.63	197	.01
	Does not assume equal	1	−10.04	2.99	−3.36	78.46	2.00
		2	−10.96	2.79	−3.92	111.58	2.00
		3	−7.00	1.73	−4.06	97.67	2.00
		4	−3.04	1.61	−1.89	96.23	1.94
		5	−3.96	1.49	−2.66	127.48	1.99

Figure 82: ANOVA with Planned Contrasts PSPP Output Window

The output window will contain four valuable tables for our analysis; Test of Homogeneity of Variances, the ANOVA table, Contrast Coefficients table, and the Contrast Test results. In our example the ANOVA result, as shown in the PSPP ANOVA table, indicates that there are statistically significant differences in the math scores based on a student's SES level, $F (2, 197) = 7.97$, $p < 0.01$.

1. The Contrasts Tests results table contains two types of results; one set of results "assumes equal variance" and the second set of results "does not assume equal variance". We will use the Levene Statistic from the Table of Homogeneity to determine which set of Contrasts results to use.

Table 28: Test of Homogeneity of Variances

	Levene Statistic	df1	df2	Sig.
math score	.14	2	197	**.87**

2. In the example the Levene Statistics IS NOT statistically significant. The Levene Statistic value does not meet our Confidence interval of 0.05. The significance for this value is actually 0.87.

3. If the Levene Statistic IS NOT statistically significant, then we use the Contrast Test results of the "assume equal variance" section. If the Levene Statistic had been statistically significant then we would have to use the "does not assume equal variance" section of the Contrasts Tests table.

4. The results table indicates that Contrasts 1, 2, 3, and 5 were statistically significant. Notice that the ANOVA with Contrasts uses the t statistic.

Table 29: Contrast Tests Results

		Contrast	Value of Contrast	Std. Error	t	df	Sig. (2-tailed)
math score	Assume equal Variances	1	-10.04	3.04	3.30	197	.00
		2	-10.96	2.87	3.81	197	.00
		3	-7.00	1.78	3.94	197	.00
		4	-3.04	1.62	1.88	197	.06
		5	-3.96	1.51	2.63	197	.01

5. Contrast 4 was not found to be statistically significant. In Contrast 4 we tested for differences in math scores between the Middle and Low SES groups. In reviewing the results, the planned contrasts test suggests that the High SES group scored significantly higher on the math scores when compared to the Middle and Low SES groups.

This result is consistent with the hypothesis found in the Confidence Intervals for the Mean, in which the mean interval for the high SES group did not overlap with the mean interval for either the low SES group or the middle SES group.

ANOVA with Planned Contrasts for Linear Trends

You may notice that the means in your data seem to exhibit a trend. The ANOVA analysis can be used to test for statistically significant linear trends between the means of our data. Below is the descriptives table for the math scores of each socioeconomic status (SES) group in our sample.

Table 30: Descriptives for Math Scores by SES

		N	Mean	Std. Deviation	Std. Error	Minimum	Maximum
math score	low	47	49.17	8.88	1.29	39.00	72.00
	middle	95	52.21	9.36	.96	33.00	75.00
	high	58	56.17	8.69	1.14	38.00	71.00
	Total	200	52.64	9.37	.66	33.00	75.00

The means of our test groups seem to follow a linear trend. A graph of the means also suggest that they have a linear trend. But is this trend statistically significant?

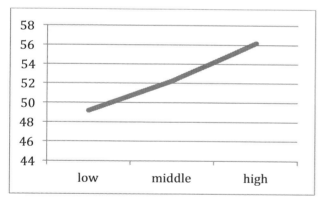

Figure 83: Math Score Means by SES

In order to test the significance of this linear trend we will use the ANOVA analysis with Contrasts. Each category in our data will be assigned a coefficient. The coefficients should generally model the linear trend, however the sum of all the coefficients must still equal zero (0).

Below is a sample contrast plan to test the data for a significant linear trend.

Figure 84: Contrast Coefficients Table

	Contrast 1
Low	2
Middle	1
High	-3

Steps to Conduct ANOVA with Contrasts for Linear Trends

1. From the PSPP menu, select Analyze > Compare Means > One Way ANOVA.

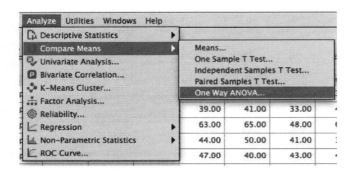

2. Move the test variable into the "Dependent Variable" window and the categories into the "Factor" window. Be sure to check both "Descriptives" and "Homogeneity" in the Statistics window.

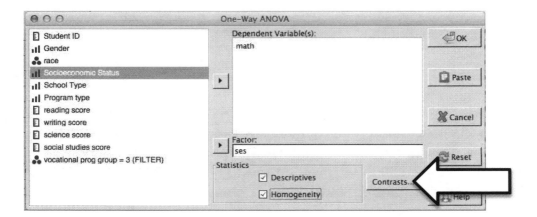

3. Click on the "Contrasts" button.

4. In the dialog window you will enter all the coefficients for your planned contrasts. The variables are entered in the same order that they were created in PSPP. In the case of our example, PSPP has the SES categories in order from Low, Middle, and High. Enter the first coefficient, then click the "Add" button. Enter the second coefficient, then click the "Add" button. Continue until all the coefficients have been entered.

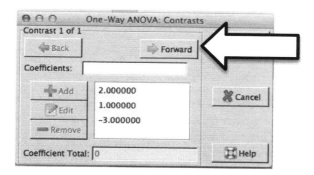

5. After the coefficients have all been entered click on the "Continue" button.

6. Click "OK" to conduct the ANOVA with Planned Contrasts analysis.

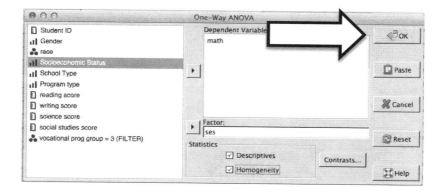

Analyzing the ANOVA Output Tables for Linear Trends

Once the ANOVA with Planned Contrasts has been conducted, go to the PSPP Output Window to interpret the results.

Test of Homogeneity of Variances

	Levene Statistic	df1	df2	Sig.
math score	.14	2	197	.87

ANOVA

		Sum of Squares	df	Mean Square	F	Sig.
math score	Between Groups	1307.09	2	653.55	7.97	.00
	Within Groups	16158.70	197	82.02		
	Total	17465.80	199			

Contrast Coefficients

	Socioeconomic Status		
	low	middle	high
Contrast 1	2	1	-3

Contrast Tests

		Contrast	Value of Contrast	Std. Error	t	df	Sig. (2-tailed)
math score	Assume equal variances	1	-17.97	4.54	3.96	197	.00
	Does not assume equal	1	-17.97	4.40	-4.08	110.20	2.00

Figure 85: ANOVA with Contrasts PSPP Output Window

The output window will contain four valuable tables for our analysis; Test of Homogeneity of Variances, ANOVA table, Contrast Coefficients, and the Contrast Test results. In our example the ANOVA result, as shown in the PSPP ANOVA table indicates that there is a statistically significant differences in the math scores based on a student's SES level, F (2, 197) = 7.97, p < 0.01, which we found in the earlier example.

1. The Contrasts Tests results table contains two types of results; one set of results "assumes equal variance" and the second set of results "does not assume equal variance". We will use the Levene Statistic from the Table of Homogeneity to determine which set of Contrasts results to use.

Figure 86: Test of Homogeneity of Variances

	Levene Statistic	df1	df2	Sig.
math score	.14		2	197	**.87**

2. In the example the Levene Statistics IS NOT statistically significant. The Levene Statistic value does not meet our Confidence interval of 0.05. The significance for this value is actually 0.87.

3. If the Levene Statistic IS NOT statistically significant, then we use the Contrast Test results of the "assume equal variance" section. If the Levene Statistic had been

statistically significant then we would have to use the "does not assume equal variance" section of the Contrasts Tests table.

4. The results table indicates that Contrasts 1 is statistically significant. Notice that the ANOVA with Contrasts uses the t statistic. So there is a significant linear trend in the math scores based on a student's SES.

Figure 87: Contrast Tests Results

		Contrast	Value of Contrast	Std. Error	t	df	Sig. (2-tailed)
math score	Assume equal Variances	1	-17.97	4.54	3.96	197	.00

5. The test for linear trends could have also been performed with the Planned Contrasts described in the previous section.

ANOVA with Planned Contrasts for Orthogonal Polynomial Trends

What is orthogonal polynomial trends? I am glad you asked. This technique merely investigates for polynomial tends in the means such as linear, quadratic, cubic, etc. We have already seen examples of investigating the relationships between the means for linear trends. The same techniques can be used to investigate trends that model other polynomial functions. The contrast coefficients are selected to model these other functions.

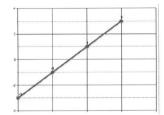 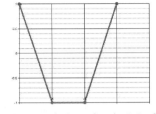 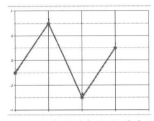

General Linear Model   General Quadratic Model   General Cubic Model

Figure 88: General Polynomial Models

The number of means or treatments contained in your data set will limit the number of trends that can be investigated. If there are 3 means present, such as was the case in our earlier example of math scores and student SES levels, they could possibly model linear or quadratic functions. If there are 4 means we could test for linear, quadratic, or cubic trends. If there are 5 means in our data set, then we could investigate for linear, quadratic, cubic, or quartic trends.

Figure 89: Trend Coefficients Model

Number of Means	Trend	Trend Coefficients
3	Linear	-1, 0, 1
	Quadratic	1, -2, 1
4	Linear	-3, -1, 1, 3
	Quadratic	1, -1, -1, 1
	Cubic	-1, 3, -3, 1
5	Linear	-2, -1, 0, 1, 2
	Quadratic	2, -1, -2, -1, 2
	Cubic	-1, 2, 0, -2, 1
	Quartic	1, -4, 6, -4, 1

In our example we will continue to use the math scores as our Dependent Variable and the student SES levels as the Factor. In the previous steps we have already discovered that the data does have a statistically significant linear trend. In this example we will investigate the differences between the means for both a linear and a quadratic trend (although from a graph of the means we have observed a general linear shape to the data).

Steps to Conduct ANOVA with Contrasts for Orthogonal Polynomial Trends

1. From the PSPP menu, select Analyze > Compare Means > One Way ANOVA.

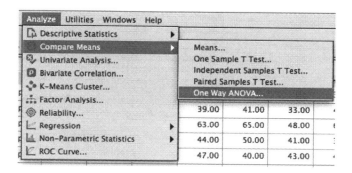

2. Move the test variable into the "Dependent Variable" window and the categories into the "Factor" window. Be sure to check both "Descriptives" and "Homogeneity" in the Statistics window.

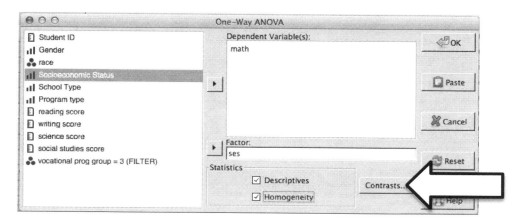

3. Click on the "Contrasts" button.

4. In the dialog window you will enter all the coefficients for your planned contrasts. The variables are entered in the same order that they were created in PSPP. In the

case of our example, PSPP has the SES categories in order from Low, Middle, and High. Enter the first coefficient, then click the "Add" button. Enter the second coefficient, then click the "Add" button. Continue until all the coefficients have been entered.

In this example we will be entering contrast coefficients to model the linear trend (-1, 0, 1) and the quadratic trend (1, -2, 1).

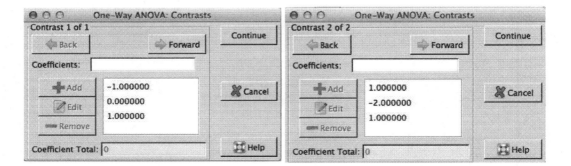

5. After the coefficients have all been entered click on the "Continue" button.

6. Click "OK" to conduct the ANOVA with Planned Contrasts analysis.

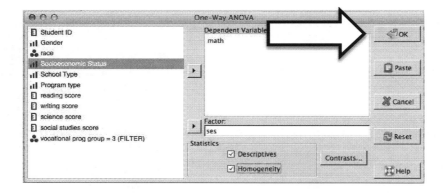

Analyzing the ANOVA Output Tables for Orthogonal Polynomial Trends

Once the ANOVA with Contrasts has been conducted, go to the PSPP Output Window to interpret the results.

Test of Homogeneity of Variances

	Levene Statistic	df1	df2	Sig.
math score	.14	2	197	.87

ANOVA

		Sum of Squares	df	Mean Square	F	Sig.
math score	Between Groups	1307.09	2	653.55	7.97	.00
	Within Groups	16158.70	197	82.02		
	Total	17465.80	199			

Contrast Coefficients

		Socioeconomic Status		
		low	middle	high
Contrast	1	−1	0	1
	2	1	−2	1

Contrast Tests

		Contrast	Value of Contrast	Std. Error	t	df	Sig. (2-tailed)
math score	Assume equal variances	1	7.00	1.78	3.94	197	.00
		2	.92	2.57	.36	197	.72
	Does not assume equal	1	7.00	1.73	4.06	97.67	.00
		2	.92	2.58	.36	188.71	.72

Figure 90: ANOVA with Contrasts PSPP Output Window

The output window will contain four valuable tables for our analysis; Test of Homogeneity of Variances, ANOVA table, Contrast Coefficients, and the Contrast Test results. In our example the ANOVA result, as shown in the PSPP ANOVA table indicates that there are statistically significant differences in the math scores based on a student's SES level, $F(2, 197) = 7.97$, $p < 0.01$.

1. The Contrasts Tests results table contains two types of results; one set of results "assumes equal variance" and the second set of results "does not assume equal variance". We will use the Levene Statistic from the Table of Homogeneity to determine which set of Contrasts results to use.

Table 31: Test of Homogeneity of Variances

	Levene Statistic	df1	df2	Sig.
math score	.14	2	197	**.87**

2. In the example the Levene Statistics IS NOT statistically significant. The Levene Statistic value does not meet our Confidence interval of 0.05. The significance for

this value is actually 0.87.

3. If the Levene Statistic IS NOT statistically significant, then we use the Contrast Test results of the "assume equal variance" section. If the Levene Statistic had been statistically significant then we would have to use the "does not assume equal variance" section of the Contrasts Tests table.

4. The results table indicates that Contrasts 1 is statistically significant. Notice that the ANOVA with Contrasts uses the t statistic. So there is a significant linear trend in the math scores based on a student's SES, as we observed in earlier examples.

In Contrast 1 we have a t-value of 3.94 which has a calculated p-value level less than 0.05, as shown in the Significance column as having a value of ".00". PSPP output tables will only show calculated p-values to two decimal places. Therefore any calculated values that appear as ".00", as displayed in our example output table above, should be reported as "p < 0.01".

Figure 91: Contrast Tests Results

	Contrast	Value of Contrast	Std. Error	t	df	Sig. (2-tailed)
math Assume equal score variances	1	7.00	1.78	3.94	197	.00
	2	.92	2.57	.36	197	.72

5. Contrast 2 for a quadratic trend is not statistically significant. The calculated p-value of ".72" is more than our significance level of p > 0.05 and the calculated t-value of 0.36 is not greater than the critical t-value from the critical values table (see Appendix).

Interpreting Output Tables: ANOVA with Contrasts (recap)

In this example we have a One-Way ANOVA analysis to determine if there are differences in the Social Studies tests scores based on a student's SES level. The contrasts are set to determine if a difference exists between the middle and high SES level students as one group and the low SES level students as the comparison group.

```
ONEWAY /VARIABLES= SocialSt BY SES
    /STATISTICS=HOMOGENEITY
    /CONTRAST= 2 -1 -1.
```

Test of Homogeneity of Variances

	Levene Statistic	df1	df2	Significance
SocialSt	.42	2	197	.66

ANOVA

		Sum of Squares	df	Mean Square	F	Significance
SocialSt	Between Groups	2528.18	2	1264.09	12.20	.00
	Within Groups	20408.01	197	103.59		
	Total	22936.20	199			

Contrast Coefficients

	SES		
	low	middle	high
Contrast 1	2	-1	-1

Contrast Tests

		Contrast	Value of Contrast	Std. Error	t	df	Sig. (2-tailed)
SocialSt	Assume equal variances	1	-14.53	3.42	4.25	197	.00
	Does not assume equal	1	-14.53	3.57	-4.07	72.78	2.00

Figure 92: ANOVA Output Table

1. The two tables that provide us with the most information are the "Test of Homogeneity of Variances" table and the "Contrasts" table.

The "Test of Homogeneity of Variances" table shows the Levene Statistic. If the Levene Statistic value is not significant, that is a significance value greater than 0.05, then we will use the first row in the "Contrast" table. If the Levene Statistic is significant, that is a significance value less than 0.05, then we use the second row in the "Contrast" table.

In this example the Levene's test is not significant so we would use the first row from the Contrast Table.

2. The ANOVA table contains an F value of 12.20 (df 2,197). This value is greater than the F critical value of 3.04, therefore the differences are significant.

3. Using the appropriate row on the "Contrast" table, we will find the t-value and the degrees of freedom (df). These values can be compared to the critical values found on the t-Test table of critical values. If the calculated value from the output table is greater than the critical value then the difference is significant and our hypothesis was accurate. In the output table we find that the t-value of 4.25 (197 df) is greater than the critical t-value of 1.98, therefore the difference is significant for the groups we selected using contrasts.

4. The "Asymp. Sig (2-tailed)" column will also give us the p-value. A value of less than 0.05 can be considered significant. The output table shows us that the p-value is less than 0.05.

Again keep in mind that the PSPP output tables will only show calculated p-values to two decimal places. Therefore any calculated values that appear as ".00", as displayed in our example output table above, should be reported as "$p < 0.01$".

5. In this example we have found that the difference in Reading scores based on a student's SES is statistically significant. Specifically that the Reading scores of the low SES student group are significantly lower than the Reading scores of the middle and high SES student groups. Now we will examine the magnitude of those differences by calculating the effect size.

The effect size for a One-Way ANOVA is the eta squared.

$$\eta^2 = \frac{SS_{between\ groups}}{SS_{total}}$$

The Sum of Squares for "Between Groups" and "Total" is taken directly from the PSPP ANOVA output table. In this example we find that the Sum of Squares Between Groups is 2528.18 and the Sum of Squares Total is 22,936.20.

$$\eta^2 = \frac{2528.18}{22936.20} = 0.11$$

The effect size magnitude table (see appendix) suggests that this is a LARGE effect. So we can conclude that the difference in reading scores between the low SES student groups does differ significantly when compared to the Reading scores of the middle and high SES student groups ($p < 0.01$) with a large effect size ($d = 0.11$).

Effect Size Calculation	Statistics Test	Small Effect	Medium Effect	Large Effect
Eta Squared	ANOVA	0.01	0.06	0.14

An effect size of 0.11 would fall in the "Large Effect" range slightly below the midpoint of the suggested range.

Chapter 10
Associations with Correlation

Correlations

The purpose of a correlation is to determine if there exists an association between two sets of data. The correlation does not take into account the various groups defined within the data, but merely tests if an association can be found.

Correlation Analysis with PSPP

1. Use the menu to select Analyze > Bivariate Correlation. This will allow you to compare two sets of continuous data for an association . The Bivariate Correlation test will perform a Pearson's Correlation on the data. Pearson's correlation is used for parametric data, as we have in this sample.

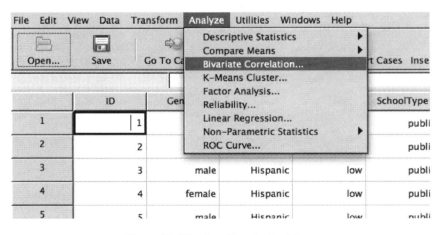

Figure 93: Bivariate Correlation Menu

2. From the dialog box move two variables into the right side column. Be sure that you have selected the two-tailed "test of significance" and check the box for "flag significant correlations".

Select the first variable from the left window then click the arrow to move this variable into the right window. Next, select the second variable to use in the correlation and click the arrow to move it to the right window.

Then click "OK".

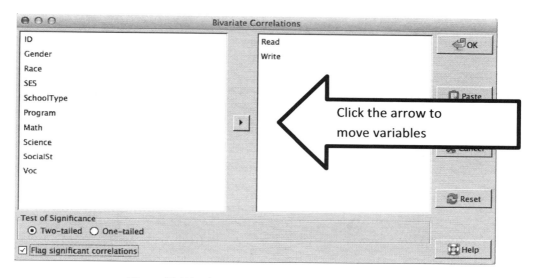

Figure 94: Bivariate Correlation Dialogue Window

3. In the Output window view the Pearson Correlation output table. The table produces rows and columns with the correlation values. The values for each corresponding comparisons in the 2 rows shown in the output table below, in this example the row with "Read" and the row for "Write", should have the same values.

```
CORRELATION
    /VARIABLES = Read Write
    /PRINT = TWOTAIL NOSIG.
```

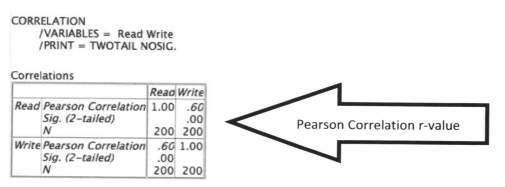

Correlations

		Read	Write
Read	Pearson Correlation	1.00	.60
	Sig. (2-tailed)		.00
	N	200	200
Write	Pearson Correlation	.60	1.00
	Sig. (2-tailed)	.00	
	N	200	200

Figure 95: Correlation Output Table

4. When examining the output table recall that correlation values range from -1 to 1, with a value of zero meaning no correlation exists. A value of -1 indicates perfect negative correlation while a value of 1 indicates perfect positive correlation. Negative correlation means that as one variable increases the other variable will decrease. Positive correlation means that as one variable increases the other variable also increases.

5. The Pearson correlation value indicates the direction and strength of the association. The second value in each row, labeled "Sig. (2-tailed)", will give the significance, or p-value, of the correlation. In the example above we could state that the variables have a positive correlation, r = 0.60, N=200, p < 0.01. The r-value can also be compared to the critical values of a Pearson r correlation coefficient table.

6. We must be careful when making statements about associations between data sets. Some of the observed correlations can be from chance while some of the correlation is due to the actual association between the data. This can be determined with a regression analysis, as discussed in the next section.

7. The r-value, as described earlier, in the correlation table can indicate the strength of the association between the variables. The closer the r-value is to 1 or -1 the stronger the association. The table below provides a general rule of thumb for judging the strength of the association.

Table 32: Correlation Strength of Relationship

r-value	Strength of Relationship
-1.0 to -0.5 or 1.0 to 0.5	Strong
-0.5 to -0.3 or 0.3 to 0.5	Moderate
-0.3 to -0.1 or 0.1 to 0.3	Weak
-0.1 to 0.1	None or very weak

8. Another valuable measure is the R-Squared value. This is calculated by squaring the r-value in the correlation output table. This value is also produced by PSPP and displayed in the output table. The R-Squared value is an indicator of the amount of variation in the dependent variable that can be explained by the independent variable.

For example, in the correlation output table shown in our example the calculated r-value is 0.60, therefore the R-Squared value would be 0.36. This would mean that 36% of the variation in writing scores could be attributed to the association between reading scores and writing scores. The R-Squared value can also be found in the Regression output table.

Interpreting Output Tables: Correlation

In this example we have a Correlation output table to determine if a association exists between the Writing scores and the Science scores. The writing test scores were input as the independent variable and the Science test scores were the dependent variable. We also have the Regression output table in this example to display the R-Squared value.

```
CORRELATION
     /VARIABLES = Write Science
     /PRINT = TWOTAIL NOSIG.
```

Correlations

		Write	Science
Write	Pearson Correlation	1.00	.57
	Sig. (2-tailed)		.00
	N	200	200
Science	Pearson Correlation	.57	1.00
	Sig. (2-tailed)	.00	
	N	200	200

REGRESSION

```
REGRESSION
     /VARIABLES= Write
     /DEPENDENT= Science
     /STATISTICS=COEFF R ANOVA.
```

Model Summary

R	R Square	Adjusted R Square	Std. Error of the Estimate
.57	.33	.33	8.15

ANOVA

	Sum of Squares	df	Mean Square	F	Significance
Regression	6347.81	1	6347.81	95.51	.00
Residual	13159.69	198	66.46		
Total	19507.50	199			

Coefficients

	B	Std. Error	Beta	t	Significance
(Constant)	20.40	3.27	.00	6.24	.00
Write	.60	.06	.57	9.77	.00

1. The correlation's r-value is found in the correlation output table (as well as the regression analysis Model Summary table). Notice that in this example the r-value between writing scores and science scores is 0.57, suggesting a moderate positive association.

Table 33: Correlation Table between Science and Writing scores

		writing score	Science score
writing score	Pearson Correlation	1.00	.57
	Sig. (2-tailed)		.00
	N	200	200
Science score	Pearson Correlation	.57	1.00
	Sig. (2-tailed)	.00	
	N	200	200

2. The regression output includes a "Model Summary" table that contains the correlation r-value as well as the R-Squared value.

Table 34: Model Summary

R	R Square	Adjusted R Square	Std. Error of the Estimate
.57	.33	.32	8.15

3. The R-Squared value of .33 suggests that the writing scores can explain 33% of the variation in the science scores. The effect size magnitude table (see appendix) suggests that this is a LARGE effect.

Effect Size Calculation	Statistics Test	Small Effect	Medium Effect	Large Effect
r^2	Correlation	0.01	0.09	0.25
r	Correlation	0.1	0.3	0.5

The calculated r-value of 0.57 for this model also suggests a large effect size between writing and science scores.

Chapter 11
Associations with Regression

Regression

The purpose of regression analysis is to explore the associations between variables and to model those associations. The analysis will tell us how much one variable changes with respect to the other variable and provide us with an equation to predict the value of one variable from the other variable. The values can also be used to model the association between the variables.

Regression Visualization with OpenOffice

1. Once we determine that an association exists, we should be able to find an equation that will allow us to use one of the variables to determine a student's predicted performance on the associated test. The values produced by a regression analysis can also model the association.

2. To visualize this linear trend create a scatterplot from the two variables. In a scatter plot the values of one variable, the independent variable, will be used for the points on the x-axis of a coordinate plane while the values of the dependent variable will be used for the points of the y-axis on the coordinate plane.

3. We can use any spreadsheet application, such as OpenOffice, to create this graphic representation of the data.

4. Launch your spreadsheet application and open the data spreadsheet. Select the two columns that contain your variables to plot. In our example we will select the reading scores and the math scores.

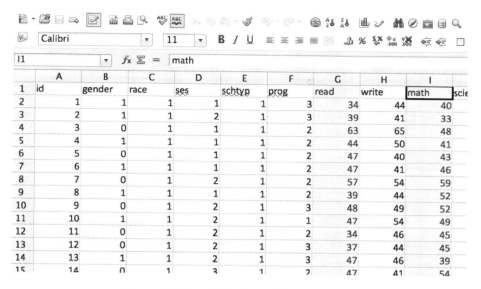

Figure 96: OpenOffice Spreadsheet of Values

5. From the menu select Insert > Chart.

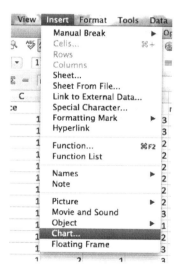

Figure 97: OpenOffice Insert Chart Menu

6. From the chart wizard dialog box select "XY (Scatter)" as the chart type. This should produce a preview chart. Here we are using OpenOffice.

Christopher P. Halter

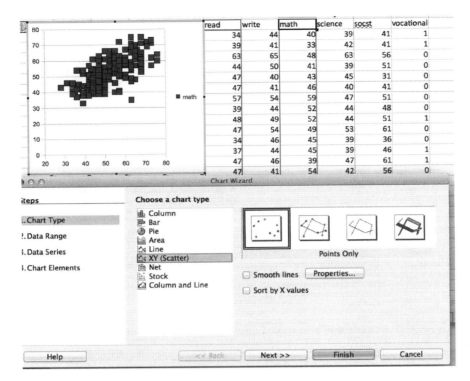

Figure 98: OpenOffice Chart Wizard Window

7. From the chart we can visually see a positive linear trend. Notice that the values on the left side of the graph are lower while the data points move upward as we move to the right side of the graph. As the x-values increase the y-values also increase.

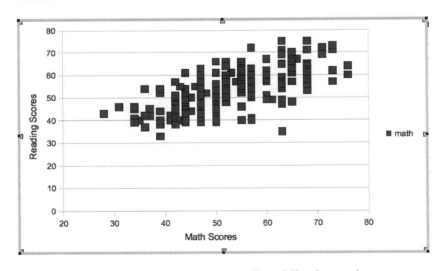

Figure 99: OpenOffice Scatterplot

120

Regression Analysis with PSPP

1. In order to perform a regression analysis, from the PSPP menu select Analyze > Linear Regression.

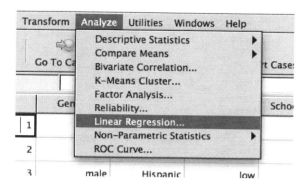

Figure 100: PSPP Linear Regression Menu

2. Using the regression dialog box move one variable into the "Dependent" box and the other variable into the "Independent" box. In this example we have used the reading score as the dependent variable and the math score as the independent variable. By doing this our hypothesis is that we will be able to predict or model a student's reading scores based on the math scores.

Select the dependent variable from the list of variables and use the selection arrow to move it into the dependent variable window. Then select the independent variable from the list and use the selection arrow to move it into the independent variable window.

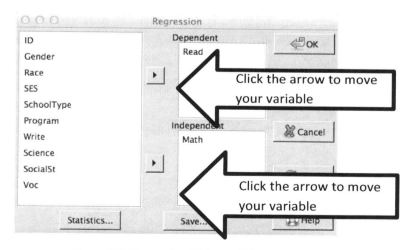

Figure 101: Regression Dialogue Window

3. Click on the "Statistics" button in the dialog box and check all the values to be displayed from the dialogue window.

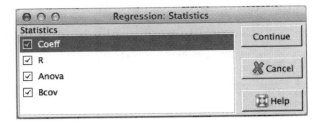

Figure 102: Regression Statistics Window

4. We will be able to examine the regression table in the output window of PSPP.

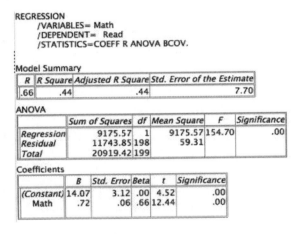

Figure 103: Regression Output Table

5. The model summary table will show the Pearson R-value that we obtained from our Bivariate Correlation, seen in the Model Summary column "R". The "R-Squared" value indicates how much of the variance is accounted for by the association. In this case we find an R-Squared value of 0.44, telling us that approximately 44% of the variance in the data is due to the association between the data sets. The higher the R-squared value the stronger the association between the data sets.

Table 35: Model Summary for Math and Reading

R	R Square	Adjusted R Square	Std. Error of the Estimate
.66	.44	.44	7.70

6. The regression output table will also produce an ANOVA table for the data. In this case we find an F-value of 154.70 (df 1,198) with a significance of p<0.01.

Table 36: ANOVA Table from Regression

	Sum of Squares	df	Mean Square	F	Sig.
Regression	9175.57	1	9175.57	154.70	.00
Residual	11743.85	198	59.31		
Total	20919.42	199			

7. The Coefficients table gives us the coefficients or the values to use in a linear equation that can be used to model the association between the dependent variable and the independent variable. The values for the linear equation are obtained from the "B" column of the coefficients output table.

Table 37: Coefficients Table

	B	Std. Error	Beta	t	Sig.
(Constant)	14.07	3.12	.00	4.52	.00
math score	.72	.06	.66	12.44	.00

8. In the example the resulting equation is;

Reading score value = 14.07 + (0.72 * math score value)

The values for this model, "14.04" and "0.72" in this example, are found in the Coefficients output table labeled "B". This linear equation suggests that if we know a student's math test score, then we multiply it by 0.72 and add 14.07, we would be able to approximate the student's expected Reading score.

In reporting a Regression analysis, we would not include the equation as part of the results. It is shown here to illustrate the predictive equation.

Interpreting Output Tables: Regression

In this example we have a Regression output table to determine the linear equation to be used to predict a student's Science test score if the student's Writing test score was known or to model the association.

```
REGRESSION
    /VARIABLES= Write
    /DEPENDENT= Science
    /STATISTICS=COEFF R ANOVA.
```

Model Summary

R	R Square	Adjusted R Square	Std. Error of the Estimate
.57	.33	.33	8.15

ANOVA

	Sum of Squares	df	Mean Square	F	Significance
Regression	6347.81	1	6347.81	95.51	.00
Residual	13159.69	198	66.46		
Total	19507.50	199			

Coefficients

	B	Std. Error	Beta	t	Significance
(Constant)	20.40	3.27	.00	6.24	.00
Write	.60	.06	.57	9.77	.00

1. It is appropriate to perform a linear regression model since the correlation table suggests that there exists a moderate positive association between our two variables.

Table 38: Correlation Table for Writing and Science scores

		writing score	science score
writing score	Pearson Correlation	1.00	.57
	Sig. (2-tailed)		.00
	N	200	200
Science score	Pearson Correlation	.57	1.00
	Sig. (2-tailed)	.00	
	N	200	200

2. The "Coefficients" table provides the values to use in a linear equation that will model the association between the variables. In this example the model was to show

the relationship between writing scores as the independent variable and science scores as the dependent variable.

Table 39: Coefficients Table (science score)

	B	Std. Error	Beta	t	Sig.
(Constant)	20.40	3.27	.00	6.24	.00
writing score	.60	.06	.57	9.77	.00

3. The values to model the linear equation can be found in the Coefficient table's column labeled "B". In this case the resulting linear equation could be written as:

Science Scores = 20.40 + (Writing scores * 0.60)

This linear equation tells us that if we know a student's writing test score we should be able to approximate the student's science score by multiply it by 0.60 and then adding 20.40.

Note that in reporting a regression analysis we would not include the equation as part of the results. It is shown here to illustrate the format that the predictive equation would take.

Chapter 12
Factor Analysis

What is Factor Analysis?

Factor Analysis is a statistical technique to take large amounts of data and reduce them to a smaller number of groups, or factors. The process makes the task of analyzing this data more manageable.

Example scenario: A researcher creates a 30-item questionnaire asking participants to rank the qualities that they find important in choosing a school for their child. Each item has a 4-point Likert scale for an item to be identified as not important to very important. The questionnaire is overwhelmingly successful and the researcher receives 450 responses. We could review the responses for each of the 30 items for all 450 participants to identify patterns and themes in the data. This may be labor intensive and can take a long time.

Factor analysis is intended to take those 30 items and reduce them into a smaller number of factors, or groups, in which the items in that group may have some relation to one another. So in the case of our example, factor analysis may be able to reduce the 30 items into a smaller number of groups that can be reviewed or analyzed.

There are two types of factor analysis:

1. Confirmatory Factor Analysis
2. Exploratory Factor Analysis

Confirmatory Factor Analysis is a method to confirm that a data collection instrument is performing as expected or designed. In designing a survey or questionnaire the researcher may have several questions that are meant to be asking about the same concept, but in slightly different ways. The expectation would be if someone responds positively to one question they would respond positively to the related question. Confirmatory Factor Analysis should group these related responses into the same groups.

Exploratory Factor Analysis is used when the data collection instrument does not have any preconceived groupings. The factor analysis procedure would group the items in factors. It is up to the researcher to analyze the groups and decide if there are any themes or connections between the items within each factor.

This chapter will deal with the procedure for Exploratory Factor Analysis.

Determining the Number of Factors to Extract

In order to conduct a useful factor analysis, we must decide on the number of factors to use so that we end up with groupings that are appropriate. There are two main methods to determine the number of factors that may be in a data set; 1) eigenvalues and 2) a scree test graph.

The eigenvalue tells us how much of the information for each group is captured by the factor. The eigenvalue table often shows a number of factors along with a percentage of the information or variability that is captured with the suggested groups.

Suppose we have a data collection instrument with 20 items. An initial factor analysis would produce the eigenvalue table shown below.

Total Variance Explained

Component	Initial Eigenvalues			Extraction Sums of Squared Loadings		
	Total	% of Variance	Cumulative %	Total	% of Variance	Cumulative %
1	3.41	17.07	17.07	3.41	17.07	17.07
2	3.21	16.06	33.13	3.21	16.06	33.13
3	1.58	7.89	41.02	1.58	7.89	41.02
4	1.37	6.86	47.88	1.37	6.86	47.88
5	1.17	5.87	53.75	1.17	5.87	53.75
6	1.16	5.78	59.53	1.16	5.78	59.53
7	.92	4.60	64.13			
8	.87	4.37	68.50			
9	.86	4.29	72.79			
10	.81	4.06	76.85			
11	.70	3.50	80.35			
12	.66	3.30	83.65			
13	.59	2.94	86.59			
14	.52	2.60	89.19			
15	.51	2.54	91.73			
16	.43	2.14	93.87			
17	.37	1.87	95.74			
18	.32	1.59	97.33			
19	.29	1.45	98.78			
20	.24	1.22	100.00			

Figure 104: Eigenvalue Table for 20-item survey

The eigenvalue table shows the number of possible components. In this case we have 20 possible groups since the survey contained 20 items. The table also displays the eigenvalues of each group and the amount of variance captured by that group, or factor. As we see in the table one factor would contain 17.07% of the possible variance within the data. As more factors are created we can account for more variance within the data until we have accounted for almost 60% of the variance with six components. This would suggest to the researcher that the data may actually contain about 6 factors.

A second method to determine the number of factors within the data would be to use a scree test. The scree test is related to eigenvalues. The test results in the graph visually represents the amount of information or variance that can be accounted for within a specific number of factors.

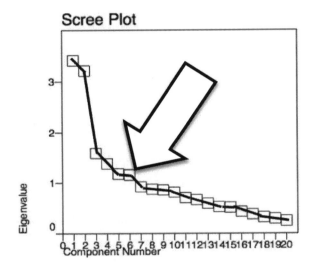

Figure 105: Scree Plot for 20-item survey

The scree plot shows the total eigenvalues contained in each factor with an increasing number of factors. As we add more factors the total eigenvalues decrease until the graph begins to flatten, indicating that less of the variance is contained within more factors.

In looking at the scree plot we are interested in the "elbow" of the graph or the point in which more factors no longer represents added benefit to the groupings. In this example we see that the graph begins to flatten after about 6 or 7 components or factors. This would suggest to us that the data may contain 6 or 7 useful factors to use in our analysis.

Between the eigenvalue table and the scree test, a researcher can select the appropriate number of factors to use in the factor analysis.

What is Factor Loading?

A Component Matrix, or factor table, is produced by the factor analysis. The columns in the table will represent the number of factors that we chose to extract from the data. Within each column is a factor load variable indicating the strength of an item's loading to other items in that specific factor.

Rotated Component Matrix

	Component					
	1	2	3	4	5	6
Q1	.71	-.01	.00	.07	-.24	-.08
Q2	.76	.08	.00	-.19	-.01	-.06
Q3	.72	-.01	-.06	.11	.12	.18
Q4	.57	-.09	-.31	.27	.30	.14
Q5	.67	.04	-.18	.11	.14	.33
Q6	.51	.21	.08	.01	-.03	.14
Q7	.13	-.05	-.20	.70	-.14	.16
Q8	.30	-.07	.15	-.20	-.18	.65
Q9	.23	-.03	.02	.29	.04	.73
Q10	.22	-.30	-.08	.14	.59	.01
Q11	-.04	.12	.26	.76	.10	-.07
Q12	-.12	.59	-.10	-.32	.29	.26
Q13	-.01	.86	.01	-.02	-.05	.04
Q14	.16	.62	.08	.01	-.04	-.28
Q15	.06	.75	.11	.17	-.08	-.09
Q16	.04	.52	.35	-.01	.05	.10
Q17	.27	.51	.29	.05	.06	-.40
Q18	-.11	.16	.10	-.14	.70	-.10
Q19	-.07	.16	.86	.04	-.05	.03
Q20	-.07	.09	.80	.01	.06	.02

Figure 106: Factor Loading Table from 20-item survey

The question we must now ask is how to interpret these loading values to determine the items that belong to a specific group. And this is not a straightforward answer.

The basic rule of thumb is that a load value of 0.40 or higher indicates that an item belongs to that factor or group. However, there are other guidelines concerning the appropriate selection of load values. But we will leave that discussion for another time.

Conducting Factor Analysis with PSPP

Step One: Determining the Number of Factors to Extract

1. To conduct a Factor Analysis using PSPP, we must first determine the number of factors to extract for analysis. Use the menu bar to select Analyze > Factor Analysis.

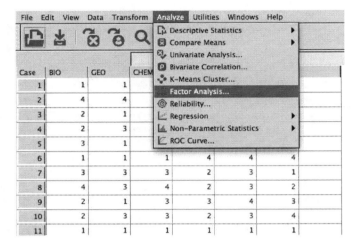

Figure 107: Factor Analysis selection

2. Move all of the necessary items into the "variables" window.

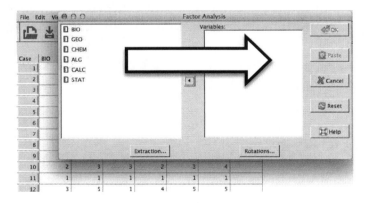

Figure 108: Factor Analysis dialog window

3. Click the "Extraction" button.

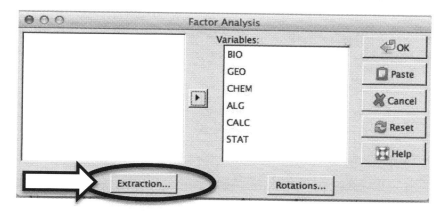

Figure 109: Factor Analysis Extraction button

4. In the dialog box for the extraction there a few changes that we need to make to the default settings.

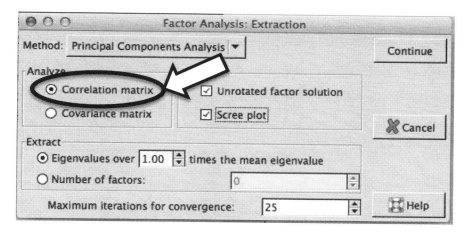

Figure 110: Extraction dialog box settings

The default setting for the method should be a Principle Components Analysis. Be sure to check the "Analyze" section to select "Correlation Matrix". All the other settings should be left on the default as shown in the figure above. Then Click "Continue".

5. The default rotation method setting for PSPP is the Varimax rotation. Rotation methods ensure that you get factors that are as different as possible. Make sure that varimax is selected by clicking the "Rotations" button and check the settings in the dialog window. Click Continue.

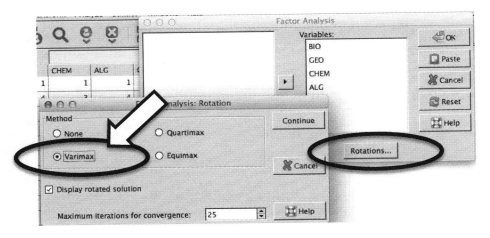

Figure 111: Varimax rotation method setting

6. Select "OK" and review the Output window.

Figure 112: Output Window selection

7. The Eigenvalue table and the scree plot can be reviewed in the output window.

Total Variance Explained

Component	Initial Eigenvalues			Extraction Sums of Squared Loadings		
	Total	% of Variance	Cumulative %	Total	% of Variance	Cumulative %
1	2.79	46.45	46.45	2.79	46.45	46.45
2	1.78	29.63	76.08	1.78	29.63	76.08
3	.63	10.51	86.58			
4	.34	5.61	92.19			
5	.26	4.37	96.56			
6	.21	3.44	100.00			

Figure 113: Eigenvalue table

The eigenvalue table suggests that we could select two factors to extract for this example analysis. This would result in accounting for approximately 76% of the variance.

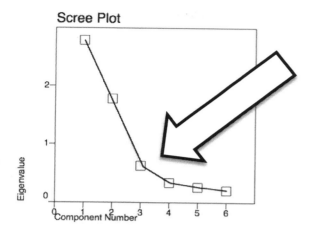

Figure 114: Scree Plot

The scree plot that is displayed for the same data suggesting that we may need three factors to account for the majority of the data. Notice that the above scree plot has a clear "elbow" at 3 components.

In our example we will choose to extract three factors based on the scree plot.

Step Two: Extracting the factors and analyzing the results

1. Now that we have determined the number of factors to use in our analysis it is time to conduct the next step in our factor analysis with the data. Using the menu select factor analysis, Analyze>Factor Analysis.

2. Move all of the necessary items into the "variables" window.

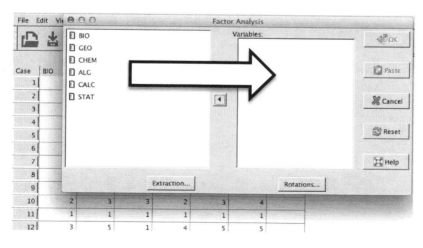

Figure 115: Factor Analysis dialog window

3. Click the "Extraction" button.

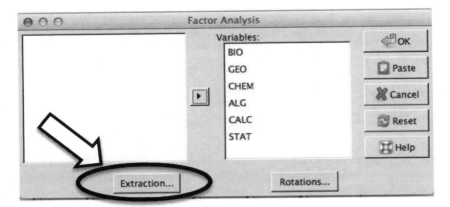

Figure 116: Factor Analysis Extraction button

4. The dialog box should be set for the default method of Principle Components. Be sure to check the analysis box for "Correlation matrix" and uncheck the display boxes for "Unrotated factor solution" and "Scree plot".

5. In the dialog box for the extraction there a few changes that we need to make to produce the useful output tables. The settings are slightly different than the ones we used to decide the number of factors to extract in Step 1. For this factor analysis step we decided to extract 3 factors, based on the scree plot. In the "Extract" section of the dialogue window, select "Number of Factors" and enter "3".

Once these settings have been selected click "Continue".

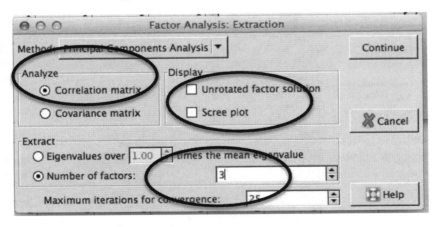

Figure 117: Settings for Extraction

6. Click the "Rotations" button and check "Varimax" for the method, then click "Continue.

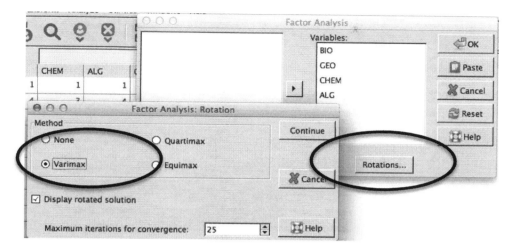

Figure 118: Varimax Selection

7. Once all the settings are selected click "OK". This will produce many tables in the output window. The most useful table will be the Rotated Component Matrix.

Rotated Component Matrix

Component

	1	2	3
BIO	.90	.09	.06
GEO	.86	.08	.12
CHEM	.91	.03	.03
ALG	.04	.94	.12
CALC	.12	.89	.26
STAT	.12	.29	.95

Figure 119: Rotated Component Matrix

8. Review the table to determine which items load to the various factors. Recall that our rule of thumb to determine which factors load to each group is to find load values greater than 0.40.

Note that this "rule of thumb" is a guideline and not an absolute rule.

In this example there are three items that load together in the first factor (BIO, GEO, & CHEM), two items that load together in the second factor (ALG & CALC), and one item that does not load to either (STAT).

Rotated Component Matrix

Component

	1	2	3
BIO	.90	.09	.06
GEO	.86	.08	.12
CHEM	.91	.03	.03
ALG	.04	.94	.12
CALC	.12	.89	.26
STAT	.12	.29	.95

Figure 120: Highlighted Rotated Component Matrix

9. The next phase of the factor analysis process would be to investigate the factors and the items contained within each to determine if there are any connections or themes that connect the items.

Once you have determined the number of factors, performed the factor analysis and decided which factors load with one another, the real work of analysis begins. The researcher would have to determine if the factors that load together have any meaning. We could look for themes or common ideas that would link the factors together. We would also look for other data that supports these themes and factor groups as having some connection.

Chapter 13
Reporting Statistics

Now that we have conducted the statistical analysis, interpreted the output tables, and have to some conclusions about our results, it is time to share these insights. Often we use the results as part of a journal article, report, white paper, course paper, thesis, or dissertation. Here we will look at statistical reporting using the American Psychological Association (APA) style guidelines.

- When including statistics in your text, be sure to provide enough information about the test so that your reader understands what was done and the rationale for that test or analysis.
- If you are using a table to display the results you do not have to repeat those results in the text. You can discuss or expand upon those results.
- You do not have to provide the formulas for common or accepted statistical methods.
- One feature you will notice in the APA-style table is that there are not any vertical lines in the table. Also the results in the table are not separated by horizontal lines.

Basic APA Style Table

Table Number
Title of Table Contents

Header			
Subheader	Column Header	Column Header	Column Header
Row 1	123	456	12.3
Row 2	789	012	45.6
Row 3	345	678	78.9

Notes that expand on the table contents would be below the table.

Tables are useful if you find that a paragraph has almost as many numbers as words. If you do use a table, *do not* also report the same information in the text. It is either one or the other, but typically not both.

Exporting Tables from PSPP to OpenOffice

The output tables created in PSPP can be easily exported. This allows you to open the tables in your word processing application and reformat the table in APA-style with the needed information.

1. Use the File > Export menu from the Output window.

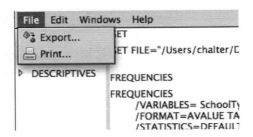

Figure 121: PSPP Export Command

2. A dialogue box will assist in the file format export process. There are several options for exporting the tables from PSPP. The OpenOffice format (.odt) is best suited to open and format the tables with a word processing application. Once the table is completed it can be copy and then pasted into any word processing application.

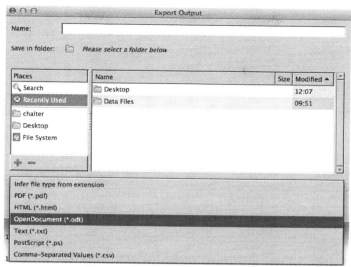

Figure 122: PSPP Export Window

3. We can also create our own tables within any word processing application, using the data from the PSPP output tables.

Exporting Tables from PSPP to Microsoft Office

The output tables created in PSPP can be easily exported to Microsoft Office as well. This allows you to open the tables in your word processing application and reformat the table in APA-style with the needed information.

1. Use the File > Export menu from the Output window.

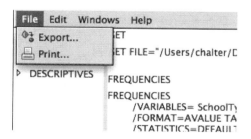

Figure 123: PSPP Export Command

2. A dialogue box will assist in the file format export process. There are several options for exporting the tables from PSPP. The HTML format (.html) is best suited to open and format the tables with the Microsoft Office word processing application. Office is capable of opening HTML files.

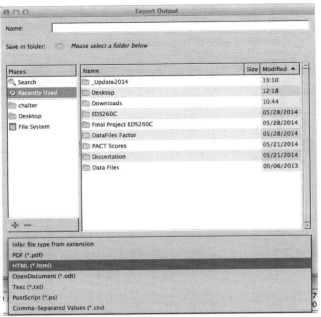

Figure 124: PSPP Export Window

3. We can also create our own tables within any word processing application, using the data from the PSPP output tables.

4. The output tables can also be exported as "HTML (*.html)" files. This option allows MS Word to work natively open the file, allowing you to copy, paste, and reformat the output tables.

Reporting Frequencies

Frequencies and descriptive statistics can be included in the text, often within parenthesis or within a table for large amounts of data.

Mean and Standard Deviation are most clearly presented in parentheses:

> The students showed similar averages on the math test ($M=52.65$, $SD=9.37$) and the science test ($M = 51.85$, $SD = 9.90$).

> The average Social Studies test score was 52.41 ($SD = 10.74$).

Percentages are also most clearly displayed in parentheses with no decimal places:

> Over three-quarters (84%) of the sample attended public school.

Sample Descriptives Tables from PSPP Output Tables

The sample reporting table uses the PSPP output table's value labels, frequencies, and percentages for the categorical data.

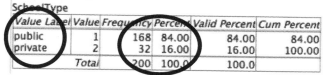

SchoolType

Value Label	Value	Frequency	Percent	Valid Percent	Cum Percent
public	1	168	84.00	84.00	84.00
private	2	32	16.00	16.00	100.00
	Total	200	100.0	100.0	

Figure 125: PSPP Screenshot School Type Frequency

Table XX

Enrollment by School Type

School Type	Frequency	Percent
Public	168	84%
Private	32	16%

Figure 126: Sample APA Formatted Frequency Table

When reporting continuous data in a table, report the measures that will be discussed within your text and have some relevance to your findings, such as number of participants, mean, standard deviation, range, maximum value, minimum value, etc.

Valid cases = 200; cases with missing value(s) = 0.

Variable	N	Mean	Std Dev	Variance	Range	Minimum	Maximum
Math	200	52.65	9.37	87.77	42.00	33.00	75.00
Science	200	51.85	9.90	98.03	48.00	26.00	74.00

Figure 127: PSPP Screenshot Math & Science Test Descriptives

Table XX

Descriptive Statistics for Math & Science Tests

Test	N	Mean	Std Dev	Variance	Range	Minimum	Maximum
Math	200	52.65	9.37	87.77	42.00	33.00	75.00
Science	200	51.85	9.90	98.03	48.00	26.00	74.00

Figure 128: Sample APA Formatted Descriptive Statistics Table

Reporting Chi Square Results

Chi-Square statistics are reported with degrees of freedom and sample size in parentheses, the Pearson chi-square value (rounded to two decimal places), and the significance level:

The percentage of enrollment by program type did not differ by gender, $\chi^2(2, N = 200) = 0.05, p = .97$.

The percentage of enrollment in public or private schools did differ significantly based on socioeconomic levels $\chi^2(2, N = 200) = 6.33, p < .05$ with a small effect size ($\phi_c = 0.13$).

Reporting t-Test Results

t-Tests are reported like chi-square results, but only the degrees of freedom are in parentheses. Following that, report the t statistic (rounded to two decimal places) and the significance level:

There was not a significant difference on math test scores based on gender, $t(198) = 0.41, p > .05$.

There was a significant difference on writing test scores based on gender, $t(198) = -3.66, p < 0.01$ with a medium effect size ($d = 0.52$).

We can also report the results of t-Test with our Confidence Intervals as well. From the results we found earlier the results would be reported as:

Using an alpha level of 0.05 an independent samples t-test was conducted to evaluate whether high SES and low SES students differed significantly on the science test. The results were statistically significant, $t(103) = 3.92, p < 0.01$ with a large effect size ($d = 0.77$). The 95% confidence interval for the science test ranged from 3.80 to 11.09. An examination of the group means indicate that high SES students (M = 55.45, SD = 9.79) performed significantly higher on the science test than did low SES students (M = 47.70, SD = 9.79).

Sample t-Test Table from PSPP Output Tables

The t-Test table should display the means and standard deviations from the "Group Statistics". The standard deviation will appear in the table in parenthesis below the mean values for each group.

The t-value as well as the degrees of freedom will also be shown in the table. The "Notes" below the table may contain the p-value and the statistical significance of the results.

Group Statistics

Gender	N	Mean	Std. Deviation	S.E. Mean
Math male	91	52.95	9.66	1.01
female	109	52.39	9.15	.88

Independent Samples Test

	Levene's Test for Equality of Variances		t-test for Equality of Means					95% Confidence Interval of the Difference	
	F	Sig.	t	df	Sig. (2-tailed)	Mean Difference	Std. Error Difference	Lower	Upper
Math Equal variances assumed	.62	.43	.41	198.00	.68	.55	1.34	-2.09	3.19
Equal variances not assumed			.41	187.58	.68	.55	1.34	-2.09	3.19

Figure 129: PSPP Screenshot t-Test Math and Gender

Group Statistics

Gender	N	Mean	Std. Deviation	S.E. Mean
Write male	91	50.12	10.31	.08
female	109	54.99	8.13	.78

Independent Samples Test

	Levene's Test for Equality of Variances		t-test for Equality of Means					95% Confidence Interval of the Difference	
	F	Sig.	t	df	Sig. (2-tailed)	Mean Difference	Std. Error Difference	Lower	Upper
Write Equal variances assumed	11.13	.00	-3.73	198.00	.00	-4.87	1.33	-7.50	-2.24
Equal variances not assumed			-3.66	169.71	.00	-4.87	1.33	-7.50	-2.24

Figure 130: PSPP Screenshot t-Test Writing and Gender

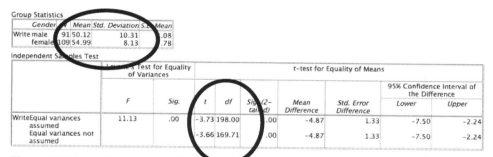

PSPP to APA

Table XX

Differences on selected Test Scores based on gender

Test	Gender		t	df
	Female	Male		
Math	52.39	52.95	.41	198
	(9.15)	(9.66)		
Writing	54.99	50.12	-3.66	169.71
	(8.13)	(10.31)		

Figure 131: Sample APA Formatted t-Test Table

Note: Differences in Math scores were not statistically significant. Differences in Writing scores were statistically significant, $p < 0.01$.

Reporting ANOVA Results

ANOVAs (both one-way and two-way) are reported like the *t* test, but there are two degrees-of-freedom values to report. First report the between-groups degrees of freedom, then report the within-groups degrees of freedom (separated by a comma). After that report the F statistic (rounded off to two decimal places) and the significance level:

> An analysis of variance showed that the effect of SES was statistically significant, $F(2, 197) = 7.97, p < .01$, on student math test scores with a medium effect size ($\eta^2 = 0.07$).

We can also report the results of a One-Way ANOVA with Post Hoc analysis.

> An analysis of variance showed that the effect of SES was statistically significant, $F(2,197) = 9.46, p < .01$, on reading test scores. Post hoc analyses indicated that the mean was significantly high in the high SES students (M = 56.50, SD = 10.86) than in the other SES groups of middle SES (M = 51.58, SD = 9.43) and low SES (M = 48.28, SD = 9.34), $t(197) = 4.21, p < .01$ with a large effect size ($\eta^2 = 0.09$).

Sample ANOVA Table from PSPP Output Tables

The ANOVA table can present your reader with a lot of data that would be difficult to read in text form. It is important to present the F-value and degrees of freedom for "between" and "within" groups analysis.

ANOVA

		Sum of Squares	df	Mean Square	F	Significance
Math	Between Groups	1307.09	2	653.55	7.97	.00
	Within Groups	16158.70	197	82.02		
	Total	17465.80	199			

Figure 132: PSPP Screenshot ANOVA Math and SES

Table XX

ANOVA Comparison of Math Test Scores by Student SES level

Variation	Sum of Squares	df	Mean Square	F	P value
Between	1307.09	2	653.55	7.97	< 0.01
Within	16158.70	197	82.02		
Total	17465.80	199			

Figure 133 Table: Sample APA Formatted ANOVA

Note: Results are statistically significant

Reporting Correlation Results

Correlations are reported with the degrees of freedom (which is $N - 2$) in parentheses and the significance level. We can also report on the direction and strength of the correlation, i.e. strong positive correlation, moderate negative correlation, etc.

The math and reading test scores had a strong positive correlation, $r(198) = .66$, $p < .01$ with a large effect size.

The science and writing test scores had a moderate positive correlation, $r(198) = .57$, $p < .01$ with a large effect size.

Sample Correlation Table from PSPP Output Tables

The correlation table is formatted to make reading the results easier for your audience. Here we show the PSPP output table formatted to reduce the data clutter.

Correlations

		Read	Write	Math	Science
Read	Pearson Correlation	1.00	.60	.66	.63
	Sig. (2–tailed)		.00	.00	.00
	N	200	200	200	200
Write	Pearson Correlation	.60	1.00	.62	.57
	Sig. (2–tailed)	.00		.00	.00
	N	200	200	200	200
Math	Pearson Correlation	.66	.62	1.00	.63
	Sig. (2–tailed)	.00	.00		.00
	N	200	200	200	200
Science	Pearson Correlation	.63	.57	.63	1.00
	Sig. (2–tailed)	.00	.00	.00	
	N	200	200	200	200

Figure 134: Screenshot Correlation of Selected Tests

PSPP to APA

Table XX

Correlation Table for Selected Tests Scores

	Reading	Writing	Math	Science
Reading	1			
Writing	.60	1		
Math	.66	.62	1	
Science	.63	.57	.63	1

Figure 135: Sample APA Formatted Correlation Table

$p < 0.01$

Reporting Regression Analysis Results

Regression results are often best presented in a table. APA doesn't say much about how to report regression results in the text, but if you would like to report the regression in the text, you should at least present the standardized slope (beta) along with the t-Test and the corresponding significance level. It is also customary to report the percentage of variance (R^2) along with the corresponding F test values.

Writing test scores significantly predicted science test scores, b = .60, $t(200)$ = 6.24, p < .01. Writing scores also explained a significant proportion of variance in science scores, R^2 = .33, $F(1, 198)$ = 95.91, p < .01.

Sample Regression Analysis Table from PSPP Output Tables

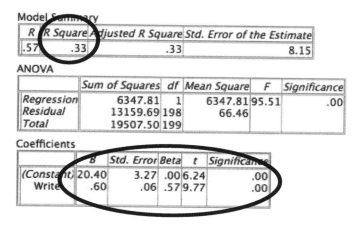

Figure 136: PSPP Screenshot Regression of Writing and Science

Table XX

Linear Regression Model of a student's Writing test scores predicting Science test scores

Variable	B	Se (B)	β	t	p-value
Writing	.60	.06	.57	9.77	<0.01

Figure 137: Sample APA Formatted Regression Table

R^2 = .33

Reporting Factor Analysis Results

In reporting Exploratory Factor Analysis results a researcher will need to explain the rationale behind the factor analysis, the reasoning for selecting the number of factors, theoretical underpinnings for the factor labels, and the factor loading table.

Theoretical underpinning

A good report will present not only the Factor Analysis results, but will also explain the theoretical underpinning of the structure of the constructs being measured. This will most likely occur in the introduction and discussion.

Type of Factor Analysis – Principal Component or Principal Axis

In the results, explain what FA extraction method was used and explain why. In our examples we will be using Principal Component Analysis (PCA). PCA is the simplest of the true eigenvector-based multivariate analyses. Often, its operation can be thought of as revealing the internal structure of the data in a way that best explains the variance in the data. What PCA does is that it takes data points and rotates it such that the maximum variability is visible. Another way of saying this is that it identifies your most important gradients or factors.

Number of Factors & Items Removed

In the results, explain the criteria and process used for deciding how many factors and which items were selected in the current data. Clearly explain which items were removed and why, plus the number of factors extracted and why. This could be through the eigenvalues table or the scree plot, or a combination.

Rotation:

In the results, explain what rotation methods were used, the reasons why, and the results. The typical method selected for rotations is varimax.

Factor Loadings

Final factor loadings should be reported in an APA formatted table. This table should also report the communality for each variable in the final column. Correlations between the factors should also be included in the report. The correlation matrix of the items may also be included so that others can re-analyse your data.

Label Factors

Meaningful names for the extracted factors should be proposed. A well-labeled factor provides a useful description of the underlying construct and helps to facilitate clarity.

Sample Report

Please note that this sample Factor Analysis report may contain more information and detail than you may typically report.

The purpose of this investigation was to explore the factor structure underlying student preference for various courses. Factor analysis has as its key objective reducing a larger set of variables to a smaller set of factors, fewer in number than the original variable set, but capable of accounting for a large portion of the total variability in the items. The identity of each factor is determined after a review of which items correlate the highest with that factor. Items that correlate the highest with a factor define the meaning of the factor as judged by what conceptually ties the items together. A successful result is one in which a few factors can explain a large portion of the total variability and those factors can be given a meaningful name using the assortment of items that correlate the highest with it.

The descriptive statistics of the item responses are presented in Table 1. It may be observed that the standard deviations are smaller than the respective means and that no one standard deviation is remarkably larger than the other variables. This indicates that our data has internal validity structure in that items line up in a predictable manner, according to what thematically ties them together conceptually.

Table 1: Descriptive Statistics

Variable	N	Mean	Std Dev
BIO	300	2.35	1.23
GEO	300	2.17	1.23
CHEM	300	2.24	1.27
ALG	300	3.05	1.17
CALC	300	3.06	1.13
STAT	300	2.94	1.26

The maximum likelihood estimation procedure was used to extract the factors from the variable data. Kaiser's rule was used to determine which factors were most eligible for interpretation because this rule requires that a given factor is capable of explaining at least the equivalent of one variable's variance. Using this rule, three factors were extracted (see Table 2). Together they are capable of explaining roughly 86.5% of all the variable variances.

Table 2: Eigenvalue Table

Total Variance Explained

Component	Initial Eigenvalues			Extraction Sums of Squared Loadings			Rotation Sums of Squared Loadings		
	Total	% of Variance	Cumulative %	Total	% of Variance	Cumulative %	Total	% of Variance	Cumulative %
1	2.79	46.45	46.45	2.79	46.45	46.45	2.41	40.14	40.14
2	1.78	29.63	76.08	1.78	29.63	76.08	1.79	29.81	69.95
3	.63	10.51	86.58	.63	10.51	86.58	1.00	16.64	86.58
4	.34	5.61	92.19						
5	.26	4.37	96.56						
6	.21	3.44	100.00						

A plot of the eigenvalues is provided below in Figure 1. A review of the initial factor loadings suggests that a reasonable solution was attainable after 3 iterations.

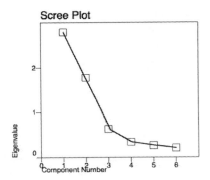

Figure 1: Scree Plot from Favorite Course Data

Communalities indicate the degree to which the factors explain the variance of the variables. Two sets of communalities are provided, the initial set and the extracted set. The values of one or more communalities do not exceed 1.00, as shown in Table 3 below, suggesting that the results are appropriate for interpretation.

Table 3: Communalities

	Initial	Extraction
BIO	1.00	.82
GEO	1.00	.77
CHEM	1.00	.83
ALG	1.00	.90
CALC	1.00	.88
STAT	1.00	1.00

Factor Loadings for the data are shown in Table 4. Principal Components Analysis with a Correlation Matrix was used in the factor analysis. Varimax rotation method was chosen. The rotated factor loading table indicates that three courses (BIO, GEO, & CHEM) load to the first factor, two courses (ALG & CALC) with the second factor, and statistics (STAT) did not have significant loading with either factor.

Table 4: Rotated Factor Component Matrix

	1	2	3
BIO	.90		
GEO	.86		
CHEM	.91		
ALG		.94	
CALC		.89	
STAT			.95

The factor loadings suggest that the way students respond to Biology, Geology, and Chemistry is very similar. There responses to Algebra and Calculus are also similar. Responses to Statistics did not relate, or load, to either of these factors.

After this point the researcher would explore other data to identify and explain these themes.

Chapter 14
Concluding Thoughts

Hopefully you have found this guide to be a useful tour through statistical analysis. There are many more methods of analysis available to us through statistics. It is up to the researcher to understand the appropriate use of these methods and to be able to select the necessary tools to answer their questions.

With descriptive statistics we are able to get a sense of the make-up and characteristics of our data. We gain information about the population demographics as well as any variation within the sample. The graphic representations, such as pie charts, histograms, and box plots allow us to visually inspect the data.

In our tests for differences within data we explored the uses of Chi Square analysis when dealing with categorical data, such as population descriptors. The t-Test uncovers differences within continuous data, such as test scores, between two groups. If we need to explore the differences within continuous data between more than two groups the ANOVA analysis can provide this information.

We are also able to determine associations between two data sets. Correlations, along with scatterplots, can point out both positive and negative associations. The strength of this association can also be measured. Once we know that an association exists, regression analysis can provide mathematical models, or linear equations, so that we can make predictions about one variable when another is known.

The true power of statistical analysis comes when we use it to provide models and uncover subtle differences within our data. Thoughtful consideration of your statistical results can lead to rich questions about the world in which we live.

Resources

Analysis Memos

The purpose of writing an analysis memo is to keep all your analyses organized and to have written documentation of all the analysis you do. This way you will know what paths you went down, which ones lead to interesting places, and you will have the writing to include in your dissertation/paper when needed.

I. Question

This is expressed in terms that can be answered with our data. (ie. Are there gender differences in responses to questions X,Y,Z?)

II. Method. (ie. summation of frequency counts, correlation, ...)

Include a rationalization for using this type of analysis if necessary.

III. Results.

Include tables and/or charts with results that could be input into formal writing if needed.

IV. Discussion.

Thoughts or reactions to results. Can be formal or informal writing.

Sample Analysis Memo

I. Question: Are there SES differences in school types?

II. Method: A chi-square test of group difference was conducted on SES, with three categories, by School type, with two categories.

III. Results: The chi-square test of group differences was significant (X^2 (2) = 6.33, p = .04), indicating that there are statistically significant group differences in SES by type of school.

Type of School by SES

School Type	SES Low	Middle	High
	N (% w/School Type)		
Public	45 (26.8%)	76 (45.2%)	47 (28%)
Private	2(6.3%)	19 (59.4%)	11 (34.4%)

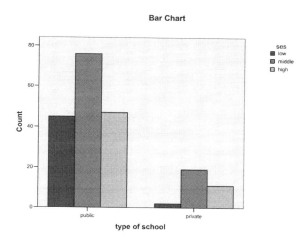

IV. Discussion: Although the majority of students from all three SES groups attend public school, fewer low income students attend private school than any other SES groups, while more middle income students attend private school than any other SES groups. This is an interesting finding as one might assume that students from high SES backgrounds would be more likely to attend private schools. I wonder if this could be due to higher SES families living in school districts with better public schools, while middle income families may not have access to the best public schools, but do have the financial means to send their children to private schools.

Chi-Square Probability Table of Critical Values

df	0.99	0.90	0.10	0.05	0.01
1	---	0.016	2.706	3.841	6.635
2	0.020	0.211	4.605	5.991	9.210
3	0.115	0.584	6.251	7.815	11.345
4	0.297	1.064	7.779	9.488	13.277
5	0.554	1.610	9.236	11.070	15.086
6	0.872	2.204	10.645	12.592	16.812
7	1.239	2.833	12.017	14.067	18.475
8	1.646	3.490	13.362	15.507	20.090
9	2.088	4.168	14.684	16.919	21.666
10	2.558	4.865	15.987	18.307	23.209
11	3.053	5.578	17.275	19.675	24.725
12	3.571	6.304	18.549	21.026	26.217
13	4.107	7.042	19.812	22.362	27.688
14	4.660	7.790	21.064	23.685	29.141
15	5.229	8.547	22.307	24.996	30.578
16	5.812	9.312	23.542	26.296	32.000
17	6.408	10.085	24.769	27.587	33.409
18	7.015	10.865	25.989	28.869	34.805
19	7.633	11.651	27.204	30.144	36.191
20	8.260	12.443	28.412	31.410	37.566
21	8.897	13.240	29.615	32.671	38.932

df	0.99	0.90	0.10	0.05	0.01
22	9.542	14.041	30.813	33.924	40.289
23	10.196	14.848	32.007	35.172	41.638
24	10.856	15.659	33.196	36.415	42.980
25	11.524	16.473	34.382	37.652	44.314
26	12.198	17.292	35.563	38.885	45.642
27	12.879	18.114	36.741	40.113	46.963
28	13.565	18.939	37.916	41.337	48.278
29	14.256	19.768	39.087	42.557	49.588
30	14.953	20.599	40.256	43.773	50.892
40	22.164	29.051	51.805	55.758	63.691
50	29.707	37.689	63.167	67.505	76.154
60	37.485	46.459	74.397	79.082	88.379
70	45.442	55.329	85.527	90.531	100.425
80	53.540	64.278	96.578	101.879	112.329
90	61.754	73.291	107.565	113.145	124.116
100	70.065	82.358	118.498	124.342	135.807

Student's t Table

df\p	0.25	0.10	0.05	0.01
1	1.000000	3.077684	6.313752	31.82052
2	0.816497	1.885618	2.919986	6.96456
3	0.764892	1.637744	2.353363	4.54070
4	0.740697	1.533206	2.131847	3.74695
5	0.726687	1.475884	2.015048	3.36493
6	0.717558	1.439756	1.943180	3.14267
7	0.711142	1.414924	1.894579	2.99795
8	0.706387	1.396815	1.859548	2.89646
9	0.702722	1.383029	1.833113	2.82144
10	0.699812	1.372184	1.812461	2.76377
11	0.697445	1.363430	1.795885	2.71808
12	0.695483	1.356217	1.782288	2.68100
13	0.693829	1.350171	1.770933	2.65031
14	0.692417	1.345030	1.761310	2.62449
15	0.691197	1.340606	1.753050	2.60248
16	0.690132	1.336757	1.745884	2.58349
17	0.689195	1.333379	1.739607	2.56693
18	0.688364	1.330391	1.734064	2.55238
19	0.687621	1.327728	1.729133	2.53948
20	0.686954	1.325341	1.724718	2.52798
21	0.686352	1.323188	1.720743	2.51765
22	0.685805	1.321237	1.717144	2.50832
23	0.685306	1.319460	1.713872	2.49987

df\p	0.25	0.10	0.05	0.01
24	0.684850	1.317836	1.710882	2.49216
25	0.684430	1.316345	1.708141	2.48511
26	0.684043	1.314972	1.705618	2.47863
27	0.683685	1.313703	1.703288	2.47266
28	0.683353	1.312527	1.701131	2.46714
29	0.683044	1.311434	1.699127	2.46202
30	0.682756	1.310415	1.697261	2.45726
inf	0.674490	1.281552	1.644854	2.32635

F Table for alpha = 0.05

df2\df1	1	2	3	4	5	6	7	8	9	10	12
3	10.13	9.55	9.28	9.12	9.01	8.94	8.89	8.85	8.81	8.79	8.74
4	7.71	6.94	6.59	6.39	6.26	6.16	6.09	6.04	6.00	5.96	5.91
5	6.61	5.79	5.41	5.19	5.05	4.95	4.88	4.82	4.77	4.74	4.68
6	5.99	5.14	4.76	4.53	4.39	4.28	4.21	4.15	4.10	4.06	4.00
7	5.59	4.74	4.35	4.12	3.97	3.87	3.79	3.73	3.68	3.64	3.57
8	5.32	4.46	4.07	3.84	3.69	3.58	3.50	3.44	3.39	3.35	3.28
9	5.12	4.26	3.86	3.63	3.48	3.37	3.29	3.23	3.18	3.14	3.07
10	4.96	4.10	3.71	3.48	3.33	3.22	3.14	3.07	3.02	2.98	2.91
14	4.60	3.74	3.34	3.11	2.96	2.85	2.76	2.70	2.65	2.60	2.53
16	4.49	3.63	3.24	3.01	2.85	2.74	2.66	2.59	2.54	2.49	2.42
18	4.41	3.55	3.16	2.93	2.77	2.66	2.58	2.51	2.46	2.41	2.34
20	4.35	3.49	3.10	2.87	2.71	2.60	2.51	2.45	2.39	2.35	2.28
30	4.17	3.32	2.92	2.69	2.53	2.42	2.33	2.27	2.21	2.16	2.09
40	4.08	3.23	2.84	2.61	2.45	2.34	2.25	2.18	2.12	2.08	2.00
50	4.03	3.18	2.79	2.56	2.40	2.29	2.20	2.13	2.07	2.03	1.95
60	4.00	3.15	2.76	2.53	2.37	2.25	2.17	2.10	2.04	1.99	1.92
70	3.98	3.13	2.74	2.50	2.35	2.23	2.14	2.07	2.02	1.97	1.89
80	3.96	3.11	2.72	2.49	2.33	2.21	2.13	2.06	2.00	1.95	1.88
100	3.94	3.09	2.70	2.46	2.31	2.19	2.10	2.03	1.97	1.93	1.85
200	3.89	3.04	2.65	2.42	2.26	2.14	2.06	1.98	1.93	1.88	1.80
>1000	1.04	3.00	2.61	2.37	2.21	2.10	2.01	1.94	1.88	1.83	1.75
df2/df1	1	2	3	4	5	6	7	8	9	10	12

df2\df1	16	20	30	40	50	60	70	80	100	200	>1000
3	8.69	8.66	8.62	8.59	8.58	8.57	8.57	8.56	8.55	8.54	8.54
4	5.84	5.80	5.75	5.72	5.70	5.69	5.68	5.67	5.66	5.65	5.63
5	4.60	4.56	4.50	4.46	4.44	4.43	4.42	4.42	4.41	4.39	4.36
6	3.92	3.87	3.81	3.77	3.75	3.74	3.73	3.72	3.71	3.69	3.67
7	3.49	3.44	3.38	3.34	3.32	3.30	3.29	3.29	3.27	3.25	3.23
8	3.20	3.15	3.08	3.04	3.02	3.01	2.99	2.99	2.97	2.95	2.93
9	2.99	2.94	2.86	2.83	2.80	2.79	2.78	2.77	2.76	2.73	2.71
10	2.83	2.77	2.70	2.66	2.64	2.62	2.61	2.60	2.59	2.56	2.54
14	2.44	2.39	2.31	2.27	2.24	2.22	2.21	2.20	2.19	2.16	2.13
16	2.33	2.28	2.19	2.15	2.12	2.11	2.09	2.08	2.07	2.04	2.01
18	2.25	2.19	2.11	2.06	2.04	2.02	2.00	1.99	1.98	1.95	1.92
20	2.18	2.12	2.04	1.99	1.97	1.95	1.93	1.92	1.91	1.88	1.84
30	1.99	1.93	1.84	1.79	1.76	1.74	1.72	1.71	1.70	1.66	1.62
40	1.90	1.84	1.74	1.69	1.66	1.64	1.62	1.61	1.59	1.55	1.51
50	1.85	1.78	1.69	1.63	1.60	1.58	1.56	1.54	1.52	1.48	1.44
60	1.82	1.75	1.65	1.59	1.56	1.53	1.52	1.50	1.48	1.44	1.39
70	1.79	1.72	1.62	1.57	1.53	1.50	1.49	1.47	1.45	1.40	1.35
80	1.77	1.70	1.60	1.54	1.51	1.48	1.46	1.45	1.43	1.38	1.33
100	1.75	1.68	1.57	1.52	1.48	1.45	1.43	1.41	1.39	1.34	1.28
200	1.69	1.62	1.52	1.46	1.41	1.39	1.36	1.35	1.32	1.26	1.19
>1000	1.64	1.57	1.46	1.40	1.35	1.32	1.30	1.28	1.25	1.17	1.03
df2/df1	16	20	30	40	50	60	70	80	100	200	>1000

High School & Beyond Codebook

Using the HSB Data file

The data file we will work with comes from the High School and Beyond (HS&B) longitudinal study (see http://nces.ed.gov/surveys/hsb/ for a more detailed overview). We will be using a small subset of this data including 200 randomly selected participants from a sample of high school students with demographic information about the students, including gender, socio-economic status, and ethnic background or race. There are also two variables that describe the school type and academic program in which the student is enrolled. Finally, this data file also contains a number of test scores on standardized tests, including mathematics, science, reading, writing, and social studies.

CODE BOOK:

Variable Name	Variable type	Variable Label	Variable Value
gender	Categorical	Gender	0=male 1=female
race	Categorical	Race	1=Hispanic 2=Asian 3=African American 4=White
ses	Categorical	Socioeconomic status	1=low 2=middle 3=high
schtyp	Categorical	School type	1=public 2=private
prog	Categorical	Program type	1=general 2=academic 3=vocation
read	Continuous	Reading score	
write	Continuous	Writing score	
math	Continuous	Math score	
science	Continuous	Science score	
socst	Continuous	Social Studies score	

High School & Beyond Sample Data Set

id	gender	race	ses	schtyp	prog	read	write	math	science	socst
1	1	1	1	1	3	34	44	40	39	41
2	1	1	2	1	3	39	41	33	42	41
3	0	1	1	1	2	63	65	48	63	56
4	1	1	1	1	2	44	50	41	39	51
5	0	1	1	1	2	47	40	43	45	31
6	1	1	1	1	2	47	41	46	40	41
7	0	1	2	1	2	57	54	59	47	51
8	1	1	1	1	2	39	44	52	44	48
9	0	1	2	1	3	48	49	52	44	51
10	1	1	2	1	1	47	54	49	53	61
11	0	1	2	1	2	34	46	45	39	36
12	0	1	2	1	3	37	44	45	39	46
13	1	1	2	1	3	47	46	39	47	61
14	0	1	3	1	2	47	41	54	42	56
15	0	1	3	1	3	39	39	44	26	42
16	0	1	1	1	3	47	31	44	36	36
17	1	1	2	1	2	47	57	48	44	41
18	0	1	2	1	3	50	33	49	44	36
19	1	1	1	1	1	28	46	43	44	51
20	0	1	3	1	2	60	52	57	61	61
21	0	1	2	1	1	44	44	61	50	46
22	0	1	2	1	3	42	39	39	56	46
23	1	2	1	1	2	65	65	64	58	71
24	0	2	2	1	2	52	62	66	47	46

25	1	2	2	1	1	47	44	42	42	36
26	1	2	3	1	2	60	59	62	61	51
27	0	2	2	1	2	53	61	61	57	56
28	1	2	2	1	1	39	53	54	50	41
29	0	2	1	1	1	52	44	49	55	41
30	1	2	3	1	2	41	59	42	34	51
31	1	2	2	2	1	55	59	52	42	56
32	1	2	3	1	3	50	67	66	66	56
33	1	2	1	1	2	57	65	72	54	56
34	1	1	3	2	2	73	61	57	55	66
35	1	1	1	2	1	60	54	50	50	51
36	1	3	1	1	1	44	49	44	35	51
37	1	3	1	1	3	41	47	40	39	51
38	0	3	1	1	2	45	57	50	31	56
39	1	3	3	1	2	66	67	67	61	66
40	0	3	1	1	1	42	41	43	50	41
41	0	3	2	1	2	50	40	45	55	56
42	1	3	2	1	3	46	52	55	44	56
43	1	3	1	1	2	47	37	43	42	46
44	1	3	1	1	3	47	62	45	34	46
45	1	3	1	1	3	34	35	41	29	26
46	1	3	1	1	2	45	55	44	34	41
47	1	3	1	1	2	47	46	49	33	41
48	0	3	2	1	2	57	55	52	50	51
49	0	3	3	1	3	50	40	39	49	47
50	0	3	2	1	1	50	59	42	53	61
51	1	3	3	1	1	42	36	42	31	39

52	1	3	1	1	2	50	46	53	53	66
53	0	3	2	1	3	34	37	46	39	31
54	1	3	1	2	1	47	54	46	50	56
55	1	3	2	2	2	52	49	49	44	61
56	0	4	2	1	3	55	45	46	58	51
57	1	4	2	1	2	71	65	72	66	56
58	0	4	2	1	3	55	41	40	44	41
59	1	4	2	1	2	65	67	63	55	71
60	0	4	2	1	2	57	65	51	63	61
61	1	4	3	1	2	76	63	60	67	66
62	0	4	3	1	1	65	65	48	63	66
63	1	4	1	1	1	52	65	60	56	51
64	1	4	3	1	3	50	52	45	58	36
65	1	4	2	1	2	55	54	66	42	56
66	1	4	2	1	3	68	62	56	50	51
67	0	4	1	1	3	37	37	42	33	32
68	0	4	2	1	2	73	67	71	63	66
69	1	4	1	1	3	44	44	40	40	31
70	0	4	1	1	1	57	52	41	47	57
71	1	4	2	1	1	57	62	56	58	66
72	1	4	2	1	3	42	54	47	47	46
73	1	4	2	1	2	50	52	53	39	56
74	1	4	2	1	2	57	50	50	51	58
75	0	4	2	1	3	60	46	51	53	61
76	0	4	3	1	2	47	52	51	50	56
77	1	4	1	1	2	61	59	49	44	66
78	1	4	2	1	2	39	54	54	53	41

79	1	4	2	1	2	60	62	49	50	51
80	0	4	3	1	2	65	62	68	66	66
81	0	4	1	1	2	63	43	59	65	44
82	1	4	3	1	2	68	62	65	69	61
83	1	4	2	1	3	50	62	41	55	31
84	0	4	2	1	1	63	57	54	58	51
85	0	4	2	1	1	55	39	57	53	46
86	0	4	3	1	1	44	33	54	58	31
87	1	4	2	1	1	50	52	46	50	56
88	1	4	3	1	2	68	60	64	69	66
89	1	4	1	1	3	35	35	40	51	33
90	1	4	3	1	2	42	54	50	50	52
91	1	4	3	1	3	50	49	56	47	46
92	1	4	3	1	1	52	67	57	63	61
93	1	4	3	1	2	73	67	62	58	66
94	0	4	3	1	2	55	49	61	61	56
95	0	4	3	1	2	73	60	71	61	71
96	1	4	3	1	2	65	54	61	58	56
97	0	4	3	1	2	60	54	58	58	61
98	1	4	1	1	3	57	60	51	53	37
99	1	4	3	1	1	47	59	56	66	61
100	1	4	3	1	2	63	65	71	69	71
101	1	4	3	1	2	60	62	67	50	56
102	0	4	3	1	2	52	41	51	53	56
103	0	4	3	1	2	76	52	64	64	61
104	0	4	3	1	2	54	63	57	55	46
105	1	4	2	1	2	50	41	45	44	56

106	1	4	2	1	3	36	44	37	42	41
107	0	4	1	1	3	47	39	47	42	26
108	0	4	2	1	1	34	33	41	36	36
109	1	4	2	1	1	42	39	42	42	41
110	1	4	2	1	3	52	55	50	54	61
111	1	4	1	1	1	39	54	39	47	36
112	1	4	2	1	2	52	59	48	55	61
113	0	4	2	1	2	44	52	51	63	61
114	0	4	3	1	2	68	65	62	55	61
115	0	4	1	1	1	42	49	43	50	56
116	1	4	2	1	2	57	59	54	50	56
117	0	4	3	1	3	34	49	39	42	56
118	1	4	2	1	1	55	62	58	58	61
119	1	4	1	1	1	42	57	45	50	43
120	1	4	3	1	2	63	52	54	50	51
121	1	4	2	1	3	68	59	53	63	61
122	1	4	2	1	2	52	59	58	53	66
123	0	4	3	1	1	68	59	56	63	66
124	1	4	1	1	3	42	54	41	42	41
125	1	4	1	1	2	68	65	58	59	56
126	0	4	2	1	1	42	31	57	47	51
127	0	4	3	1	2	63	59	57	55	56
128	0	4	3	1	2	39	33	38	47	41
129	1	4	1	1	1	44	44	46	47	51
130	1	4	3	1	1	43	54	55	55	46
131	1	4	3	1	2	65	59	57	46	66
132	0	4	2	1	2	73	62	73	69	66

133	0	4	2	1	3	50	31	40	34	31
134	0	4	1	1	1	44	44	39	34	46
135	1	4	1	1	2	63	60	65	54	66
136	0	4	2	1	2	65	59	70	63	51
137	1	4	3	1	2	63	65	65	53	61
138	1	4	2	1	3	43	57	40	50	51
139	1	4	2	1	2	68	59	61	55	71
140	0	4	2	1	3	44	41	40	50	26
141	0	4	3	1	3	63	44	47	53	56
142	1	4	2	1	3	47	42	52	39	51
143	0	4	2	1	3	63	63	75	72	66
144	0	4	3	1	1	60	65	58	61	66
145	1	4	2	1	3	42	46	38	36	46
146	0	4	3	1	2	55	62	64	63	66
147	1	4	1	1	2	47	62	53	53	61
148	1	4	2	1	3	42	57	51	47	61
149	0	4	1	1	1	63	49	49	66	46
150	0	4	2	1	3	42	41	57	72	31
151	1	4	2	1	3	47	46	52	48	46
152	1	4	3	1	2	55	57	56	58	61
153	0	4	2	1	3	39	31	40	39	51
154	0	4	3	1	2	65	65	66	61	66
155	0	4	2	1	1	44	44	46	39	51
156	1	4	2	1	2	50	59	53	61	61
157	0	4	2	1	1	68	59	58	74	66
158	1	4	2	1	1	52	54	55	53	51
159	0	4	3	1	2	55	61	54	49	61

160	1	4	2	1	2	55	65	55	50	61
161	1	4	1	1	2	57	62	72	61	61
162	1	4	2	1	3	57	52	40	61	56
163	1	4	1	1	2	52	57	64	58	56
164	0	4	2	1	3	31	36	46	39	46
165	0	4	1	1	3	36	49	54	61	36
166	1	4	2	1	2	52	59	53	61	51
167	0	4	2	1	1	63	49	35	66	41
168	0	4	2	1	2	52	54	57	55	51
169	0	4	1	1	1	55	59	63	69	46
170	0	4	3	1	2	47	62	61	69	66
171	0	4	2	1	2	60	54	60	55	66
172	0	4	2	1	2	47	52	57	53	61
173	1	4	1	1	1	50	62	61	63	51
174	0	4	2	2	2	68	59	71	66	56
175	1	4	3	2	1	36	57	42	50	41
176	0	4	2	2	2	47	47	41	42	51
177	0	4	2	2	2	55	59	62	58	51
178	0	4	2	2	3	47	57	57	58	46
179	1	4	2	2	2	47	65	60	50	56
180	1	4	3	2	2	71	65	69	58	71
181	0	4	2	2	2	50	46	45	58	61
182	1	4	2	2	2	44	52	43	44	51
183	0	4	2	2	2	63	59	49	55	71
184	1	4	2	2	3	50	52	53	55	56
185	0	4	2	2	2	63	57	55	58	41
186	1	4	2	2	2	57	62	63	55	41

187	1	4	2	2	1	57	41	57	55	52
188	1	4	3	2	2	63	62	56	55	61
189	0	4	2	2	2	47	59	63	53	46
190	1	4	2	2	2	47	59	54	58	46
191	1	4	3	2	2	47	52	43	48	61
192	0	4	3	2	2	65	67	63	66	71
193	1	4	2	2	2	44	49	48	39	51
194	1	4	3	2	2	63	63	69	61	61
195	0	4	2	2	1	57	57	60	58	56
196	0	4	3	2	2	44	38	49	39	46
197	0	4	3	2	2	50	42	50	36	61
198	1	4	3	2	2	47	61	51	63	31
199	0	4	3	2	2	52	59	50	61	61
200	0	4	2	2	2	68	54	75	66	66

Effect Size Tables

Effect Size Magnitude Table

Effect Size Calculation	Statistics Test	Small Effect	Medium Effect	Large Effect
Phi or Cramer's Phi	Chi Squared	0.1	0.3	0.5
Cohen's d	t-Test (Paired & Independent)	0.2	0.5	0.8
Eta Squared	ANOVA	0.01	0.06	0.14
r	Correlation	0.1	0.3	0.5
r^2	Correlation and t-Test (Independent)	0.01	0.09	0.25

Values from Cohen (1988) Statistical Power Analysis for the behavioral Sciences

Effect Size Calculation Equations

Effect Size Calculation	Statistics Test	Equation	Notes
Phi (φ)	Chi Squared 2X2	$\varphi = \sqrt{\dfrac{\chi^2}{N}}$	N is the total number of observations.
Cramer's Phi (φ_c)	Chi Squared > 2X2	$\varphi_c = \sqrt{\dfrac{\chi^2}{N(k-1)}}$	N is the total number of observations and k is the lesser of rows or columns.
Cohen's d	t-Test (Paired)	$d = \dfrac{mean_2 - mean_1}{standard\ deviation\ (SD)}$	
Cohen's d	t-Test (Independent)	$d = \dfrac{mean_2 - mean_1}{SD\ pooled}$	SD pooled = $\sqrt{\dfrac{(SD_{group1})^2 + (SD_{group2})^2}{2}}$
Eta Squared	ANOVA	$\eta^2 = \dfrac{SS_{between\ groups}}{SS_{total}}$	
r	Correlation and t-Test (Independent)	$r = \sqrt{\dfrac{t^2}{(t^2+df)}}$	Correlation output tables will show the r-value.
r^2	Correlation and t-Test (Independent)	$r^2 = \dfrac{t^2}{(t^2+df)}$	Correlation output tables will show the r^2-value.

Additional Resources

PSPP

PSPP Homepage
http://www.gnu.org/software/pspp/pspp.html

PSPP Installer Listing
http://www.gnu.org/software/pspp/get.html

Online Statistics Reference

Research Methods Knowledge Base
http://www.socialresearchmethods.net/kb/index.php

CSU San Marcos ANOVA information and resources
http://www.csusm.edu/psychology/statistics_help/anova.html

Statistics Help for Students
http://statistics-help-for-students.com/

UCLA Statistical Analysis Decision Maker
http://www.ats.ucla.edu/stat/stata/whatstat/whatstat.htm

Free Statistical Software Listing
http://statpages.org/javasta2.html

Reporting Statistics in APA Style Guide
http://my.ilstu.edu/~jhkahn/apastats.html

Statistical Tables (Chi Square, t-test, F distribution)
http://www.medcalc.org/manual/statistical_tables.php

DissertationStatistics.com Reference Guide
http://www.dissertation-statistics.com/statistical-tests.html

Online Statistical Calculators

ANOVA Calculator
http://www.physics.csbsju.edu/stats/anova.html

Tukey's Post Hoc calculator
http://web.mst.edu/~psyworld/tukeys4mean.htm

QuickCalc Post-Test calculators
http://graphpad.com/quickcalcs/posttest1.cfm

Inter-rater Reliability Calculator
http://www.med-ed-online.org/rating/reliability.html

Textbook Resources

Hinton, P. (1995). *Statistics Explained: A Guide for Social Science Students* (2nd ed.). Routledge.

Hinton, P. (2004). *Statistics Explained: A Guide for Social Science Students, 2nd Edition* (2nd ed.). Routledge.

Hinton, P., Brownlow, C., & McMurray, I. (2004). *SPSS Explained* (1st ed.). Routledge.

Koosis, D. J. (1997). *Statistics: A Self-Teaching Guide* (4th ed.). Wiley.

Salkind, N. J. (2010). *Statistics for People Who (Think They) Hate Statistics* (Fourth ed.). Sage Publications, Inc.

Salkind, N. J. (2011). *Study Guide to Accompany Neil J. Salkind's Statistics for People Who (Think They) Hate Statistics, 4th Edition* (4 Stg.). Sage Publications, Inc.

Sample Data Resources

Data used in the PSPP Guide
http://creativemindspress.weebly.com/resources-for-pspp.html

Other available data sets
http://www.hlm-online.com/datasets/

Index

ABOUT THE AUTHOR

Christopher P. Halter, Ed.D, is a faculty member at the University of California San Diego's Department of Education Studies. He teaches courses in mathematics education, secondary mathematics methods, research methodology, emerging technologies, and statistical analysis. His research includes teacher development, new teacher assessment, digital storytelling, and video analysis. He also teaches online courses in creating online collaborative communities, middle school science strategies, and blended & synchronous learning design.

Made in the USA
Lexington, KY
19 August 2015